That spot of my birth has no equal on Earth
Mount Massey the Flower of Macroom
And it's you I'll invite, where I first saw the light,
In Mount Massey the Flower of Macroom

Irish Examiner/Evening Echo

Copyright © onstream

Text copyright © Roz Crowley

ISBN: 978 1 897685 56 3

Published in Ireland 2016 by Onstream, Currabaha, Cloghroe, County Cork, Ireland.

www.onstream.ie

Author: Roz Crowley

Front cover: Rory Gallagher on stage: Cork Examiner/Evening Echo.
Back cover: Paul Roberts Sniff 'n'The Tears: Cork Examiner/Evening Echo

Editorial team: Siobhan Cronin, Lia Curtin

Book design and production: Nick Sanquest

Printing: KPS Colour Print

MACROOM MOUNTAIN DEW

MEMORIES OF IRELAND'S FIRST ROCK FESTIVAL

Roz Crowley

Foreword John Martin Fitz-Gerald

Hughie Flint of The Blues Band *Irish Examiner/Evening Echo*

Contents

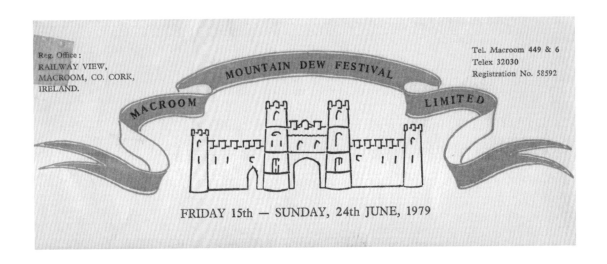

Reg. Office:
RAILWAY VIEW,
MACROOM, CO. CORK,
IRELAND.

Tel. Macroom 449 & 6
Telex 32030
Registration No. 58592

MACROOM MOUNTAIN DEW FESTIVAL LIMITED

FRIDAY 15th — SUNDAY, 24th JUNE, 1979

Foreword

Forty years ago the sleepy rural town of town of Macroom came to life in a way like never before. In these pages you will read how the Macroom Mountain Dew Festival came about and who made it happen. Each contributor to its success deserves credit for being part of what was considered an unlikely event for such a conservative town. It would be impossible to credit everyone involved, but those left out can bask in the reflected glory, and in the next edition will have an opportunity to have their say.

Based on its voting patterns, Macroom would be considered a 'traditional' or 'conservative' or even 'predictable' town. At least it was back then. So apart from the rocks that a millennium ago created the cooking sites at Codrum, the wedge tombs, standing stones, dolmens and burial sites throughout the hinterlands of the town, Rock was not a word associated with Macroom. But that was all turned around when a group of us got together in desperation. In 1976 the town was on its knees. There were few businesses prospering, many just surviving, with little inward investment and plenty of stagnation. It wasn't the only town in Ireland to suffer in this way, and fortunately, enough Macroom people were wise enough to recognise the situation. When a group of us got together, a synergy was created. Ideas were bounced around and a music festival was the one which kept its momentum.

The very idea of a music festival seemed to appeal to us twenty- and thirty-somethings who had flashes of reckless abandon and wild carefree nights, and maybe it was best that we didn't over-think it. There was no template for big concerts in Ireland back then and even less knowledge of large open-air ones. The skillset of the committee included resourcefulness and on-the-hoof problem-solving when you didn't have the luxury of meetings to discuss and debate. But there were still plenty of weekly meetings held throughout the year, long before the festivals started. And plenty of people who were well organised, creating spreadsheets, to-do lists, budgets – a reflection of the accountants, engineers and business people on the team. If we appeared casual to those telling their stories in this book, we can admit now that we were more like ducks gliding along the river, paddling like hell underneath.

In this book you will read some amusing stories from a wide range of contributors who attended and performed at the festival over its seven years. While many gave endless hours of their time, and were supported by their partners, like my own late wife Margaret (who had a number of roles throughout the years of the festival), I have yet to find anyone who regrets that time they gave.

Many of us still miss our Chairman, the late Denis Murphy, without whom the festival would not have happened at all. He had a selfless sense of community and social responsibility and a generosity of spirit second to none. At the same time he rolled his sleeves up, leading from the front at any time of the day or night. He would be delighted to read some of the comments in this book such as, "The town will never be the same", and referring to big concerts which followed – "Imagine this all happened because of Macroom".

I am glad my son Bill goaded me into getting this book underway. He was tired of being asked about the festival, how it came into being, who performed at it and why it ended. His siblings Jackie, Karen, Jennifer, Dan and John agreed I should get on with it. I started to write it myself, and with help from Frank Hanover – who was referred to me by Ronnie McGinn – we put some facts together to present to Roz Crowley who completed the work. My thanks to my partner Breeda for moving it on to that stage and to the O'Callaghan brothers, John and Donal, and to Pat O'Connell and Pat Kelleher for sharing their well-preserved records which have been used in these pages. Once again this book proves that people who are prepared to share their assets can be part of something that is greater than the sum of its parts. This is your celebration.

John Martin Fitz-Gerald, May 2016

Dedicated to the memory of Denis Murphy, Festival Chairman

Irish Examiner/Evening Echo.

1. From Standing Stones to Rock & Roll: The Transformation of Macroom

"Bring it on! Bring business to our town and put it on the map!" A group of the sons of Macroom agreed. The town needed activity. It needed to find some way of creating a sustainable venture that would nurture and benefit its inhabitants. The town, a mere 24 miles from an international airport, sea port, and railway station, had potential for international investment. Local businesses needed a confidence boost too.

A gateway to the west, it was just a place to stop for an ice-cream, a loaf of bread and slices of cooked ham, for a day out in Killarney. The town needed a bit of a shake, rattle and roll to tempt, not just international investors, but Irish people to rest there for longer. Something was needed to energise, amuse and entertain the local population. A Rock concert fitted the bill. It could profess to be Ireland's first Rock festival and the first open-air concert of that magnitude in the country. Big claims for what would change forever the way music was enjoyed in Ireland. And at the end of it all, would leave the world, or at least Macroom, a better place.

A music festival in the town of Macroom, with a population of 3,000, west of Cork and east of Kerry, was innovative for sure. With limited beds, but decent space in the Castle grounds and from other willing space providers, crowds could be catered for with camping facilities. They would not require luxury, just space to lay their heads.

Evolving during one late-night meeting, a distillation of other meetings, fuelled by more than a few pints of beer, the idea of a Rock concert was crowned with the kind of youthful enthusiasm that overcomes obstacles.

One small idea became big. And the next day over breakfast the idea still seemed like a good one, growing from just Rock to embrace a wider range of musical genres. Records showed Macroom had the lowest rainfall in June in the previous 100 years, so it was chosen as the best month to hold an outdoor festival. The Dome could be brought from the Rose of Tralee to accommodate much larger numbers than the existing theatre and hotels. Holding 1,500 sitting and 3,000 standing/dancing, it might just be large enough for the plan.

A few meetings later and lists had been

made with minutes written up. Budgets were created. Timescales worked out. Tasks delegated. There would be music in Macroom to beat all. Thinking big was not a problem. A mission statement was established: To leave the town no less, but greater, better and more beautiful than it was before us.

Mountain Dew, a potent distillate of the Macroom hinterland, was a good match for potent music. Used to warm the cockles, as a liniment for horses – whatever ails you – the name was suggested by local journalist, the late Pat Lynch, and it stuck. The Macroom Mountain Dew Festival was an organic appellation. No need for additives.

Ireland had a tradition of open-air concerts. Fleadhs held countrywide were always joyous and there was never a shortage of talent. In rural areas postcard pictures were created when any hint of fine weather brought out the tin whistle played by someone sitting on a chair outside their door. Dancing at the crossroads was long gone, and with it a filmic image of innocence, a tough, simple life. Ireland in the sixties and seventies instead embraced Rock 'n' Roll, The Beatles, blues, The Rolling Stones, showbands. Trad music still survived and prospered. But now punk beckoned.

The team looked around. Outdoor concerts had been held in the US. In 1969, Woodstock had become legendary. Glastonbury had started its two-day festival in 1970 on a small scale, offering free milk from its farm in Somerset in south west England. It grew to the five-day event it is today. There was plenty for the Macroom team to consider.

The members of the board of directors had a massive task ahead of them in getting the people of Macroom involved. It was a conservative town, not open to new ideas. Bordered by the Sullane River, a tributary of the River Lee, it was happy just the way it was. Attempts at change were not embraced. To bring all sides together, there should be community activities for the town's 3,000 inhabitants. Something the whole town could enjoy, no matter what age. A proper, well thought out community festival. The town had to be behind it, and if all went to plan, profits would go towards new equipment for the playground.

The board had varied talents, but none of them had the kind of experience required for hosting an event of the magnitude that would subsequently emerge. However, what they did have was business savvy. They knew enough to form a limited company, so from the start the festival was on a sound footing. Sprinkled with a little Mountain

POUNDS X1000

24
22
20
18
16
14
12
10
8
6
4
2

-2
-4
-6
-8
-10
-12
-14

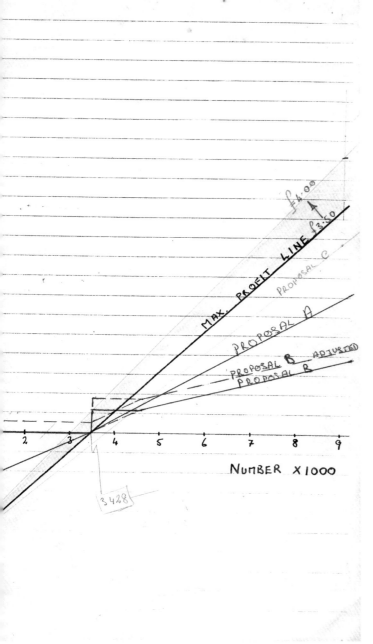

MAX. PROFIT LINE £3.50

£4.00

£3.50

PROPOSAL C

PROPOSAL A

PROPOSAL B ADJUSTED

PROPOSAL B

2   3   4   5   6   7   8   9

NUMBER X 1000

3428

Dew, the magic was ignited.

Ted Cotter, Tom Counihan, Maurice Cullen, John Martin Fitz-Gerald (Fitzie), Pat Kelleher, Michael Lynch, Anthony Murphy, Matt Murphy, Brendan O'Brien, Donal O'Callaghan and his brother John, and Pat O'Connell formed the board of directors with the late Denis Murphy as Chairman completing the baker's dozen that would run the festival. Later a ladies' committee was created to run alongside it.

There were echoes of Woodstock here. Held in farmlands in Bethel, a town outside New York, it had been an ambitious event aimed at raising funds for a recording studio. It lasted just one year. The concert attracted crowds far beyond the anticipated numbers, and entry points and ticketing were impossible to control. Organisers gave up and let everyone in free. As soon as it was over, the farmer whose field was used, went back to dairy farming and refused a second year, so recouping losses by holding another concert on the same site was not possible. Other locations failed to take hold, but a movie of the extraordinary happening was distributed worldwide and covered the debt. Glastonbury had embraced a mix of music cultures and forty-five years on, is still going strong.

In 1976, Ireland had just one national

Pot still arriving *Denis Minihane, Cork Examiner/Evening Echo*

television channel, with the powerful influence that lack of choice brings. Eurovision had taken hold with Red Hurley representing Ireland with the song 'When' which he would sing many times during the night of 23rd June in The Dome. *The Late Late Show* was the most powerful influence, with plenty to talk about on Monday mornings. Marianne Faithfull appeared on it the night before her appearance in The Dome in Macroom, and that was just what the festival needed. But the print media were essential for further promotion.

Macroom seemed like a good enough location for a Rock concert. While not on a direct train route, since the closure in 1953 of the Cork-Macroom Great Southern Railway line, it was within easy driving distance of Cork Airport and railway station, with a bus service that was usually sufficient for commuters. The town is impressive to approach from the east. A long street leading to a square with a backdrop of a crenellated gateway into the Castle grounds, a dip down to the river, a bend to the left, up the hill and you could head for Ballyvourney, awash with Irish cultural heritage, and on to Kerry.

Macroom has an interesting history with the Castle grounds as its centrepiece. This had a sad provenance, having been burned down a number of times, most recently at the outbreak of the Civil War in 1922. Once resplendent and replete, the building ended up derelict, the manicured lawns a forgotten beauty.

In his book *Memories of Macroom* author James Kelleher tells of the enterprising and practical residents of Macroom approaching RC Williams of William's Hotel and Coolcower House to contact his fellow landowner Lady Ardilaun – Olivia Hedges-White – who was born at Macroom Castle in 1850. Her father was the second son of the first Earl of Bantry. She married Sir Arthur Edward Guinness in 1871. He died in 1915 with no heirs. A proud descendent of the original MacCarthy family, Lady Ardilaun reluctantly gave up Macroom Castle, which she had inherited from her father. The purchase of the demesne was concluded by RC Williams (known as 'Dickie') and Jeremiah O'Leary, with the offer of £1,500 on one condition: that a golf course be put in place. A meeting of sixteen business people (TM Cronin, Patrick Crowley, JM Fitzgerald, Dr Mortimer Kelleher, T. Lucey, Denis Lynch, ML McSweeney, Henry Murphy Dr P.O'Donoghue, P O'Keefe, Cors O'Leary, Jerh O'Leary, John O'Shea, M. Purcell, TJ Twomey, RC Williams) honoured the proviso and agreed that each of them would donate £100 for its purchase (with enough spare to deal with problems). The deal was done, and later the western part of the estate was bought by Murt Twomey of Rockboro for £1,500. In 1925, the remainder of the grounds became the property of the sixteen trustees for the benefit of the people of Macroom. It seems the Mountain Dew Festival was not the first time the people of Macroom worked together with a common purpose.

The property had a natural amphitheatre, usually used for GAA matches, and proved to be ideal for the second year of the festival when, to accommodate Rory Gallagher's legion of fans, the main musical events were held in the open-air. It was to give birth to a new culture of entertainment, a new way of bringing fans together in vast numbers to enjoy their musical heroes.

The festival would offer something to keep people in the market town, to expose its topographic and historical features whilst selling beds, beer and burgers.

Cork Examiner/Evening Echo

Rory Gallagher *John Sheehan*

2. Reaching for the Stars

Members of the board had experience in booking music acts for their youth club and for some of the pubs. When they thought of inviting Marianne Faithfull, they knew they were reaching for the stars, but refusal was never going to be taken personally. When she accepted and the date was in the diary, the first Mountain Dew Festival took off. The wheels were in motion. There was no going back. It would span two weekends, with main acts to attract the working/ student population from inside and outside Macroom, and plenty of entertainment during the week in The Dome with free concerts out of doors.

The festival needed the goodwill of the townspeople. Businesses needed to be informed; residents kept in the loop. For many it didn't take too much persuasion. In 1976, the first year of the festival, Ireland had a bank strike, releasing cash for some who spent 'on credit'. But 1973 oil price hikes meant that inflation was steadily climbing. In spite of this, or perhaps because of it, Macroom was determined to bring business into the town, to self-heal, and make the best of its resources. And it had many. Its people proved to be it greatest asset. A dynamic Junior Chamber of Commerce had active members willing to take a chance, along with enthusiastic community and youth club members.

Businesses were curious about the first festival in 1976, but when, for the 1977 one – the first outdoor festival – Rory Gallagher was announced as the main attraction, a small percentage of them, like snails, drew themselves into their shells. Shops boarded up their premises, wary of the type of rocker who would follow the nation's idol. There was fear of smashed windows, trampling of gardens, lack of respect for property. All those people converging on their town! The locals may have thought they had reason to worry, but the people attracted to the Mountain Dew Festival were there for the music. The sea of denim signified the appreciation of guitar chords, mastery of instruments, voices, manual dexterity and musicality.

Raw expression of varied music styles was revered by fans who recognised talent. And, in the case of Rory Gallagher, they craved the best kind of talent: homegrown. He was theirs, and the fact that he was born in Ballyshannon (fittingly, in 'Rock Hospital') took little away from the fact that, as he often proudly stated in interviews, he grew up in Cork. His mother, born Monica Roche,

was from down the road in Ballyvourney.

The festival directors were keen to have a mix of homegrown talent, local, national and big international names to draw the crowds. In 1976 there was dancing in The Dome to bands such as The Nevada with Ronnie Medford and Tina, The Premier Aces, Dermot O'Brien with guest star Cathal Dunne, Red Hurley, Crúibín and Harp, The Freshmen, Horslips, and in concert Julie Felix. A ceilí was held in the Castle ballroom.

Add to that a mix of events, from fashion shows to 'glassy allie' matches, and you find what they were aiming for: something for everyone. The Montreal Olympics were held this year and prompted a surge of physical activity. June was a perfect month to get everyone out.

Getting all of the town involved was important to the organisers. Traditional activities needed to be interspersed with new attractions that would draw out the curious amongst them.

Traditional music and dancing and talent competitions would contrast with pig races, which started out from Railway View at the eastern part of the town, with the finishing line at the Castle gates.

For those interested in other traditions, there would be an old time parade, pony and trap procession, butter making, spinning

wheels, penny farthing bikes, horse and pony races, a drag hunt, pony trotting, a fancy dress parade, flower shows, a strawberry fête, treasure hunts, baby shows, brass band performances, classical music concerts, and history lectures.

To top it all the Festival Ball, open to everyone, would be held each year in Coolcower House bringing Macrompians together to enjoy each other's company without the pressure of the festival operations.

Macroom was ready for the task, with crowds catered for by providing camping spaces in addition to a range of hotel and bed and breakfast accommodation. Performers had to be catered for too, and as well as Coolcower House and the Castle and Victoria hotels in the town, McEgan College was opened up to provide catering space for acts playing throughout the festival. Complex contracts drawn up by demanding managers usually called for meals, alcohol and a general minding of their precious clients. It all had to be put in the mix.

The town was once a meeting place for the Druids of Munster, where gods, including Crom after which the town is named, were worshipped. In their place, musical deities would inspire music lovers from all over the country to get to Macroom.

The directors built their impressive programme. No-one had a fortune to spend, so ticket prices were kept low in the hope that attendance numbers would be high. As the years went on, weekend tickets were created to give people the best possible value. Ticket prices were negotiated with agents too, as acts would share in sales, often on a 60/40 basis in favour of the act, usually with a guaranteed minimum attendance fee. Tickets for Marianne Faithfull's gig were released at a very reasonable £2 a ticket and,

as a result, sales rocketed. It was all part of the business of the festival.

In a break from the norm of other major festivals, it was decided that everyone – performers and festival-goers – would be treated equally. There would be no hospitality areas for the élite to gather with sponsors in glamorous fenced-off marquees. Festival headquarters were to be located at Denis Murphy's office over his Spar shop at Railway View, and Martin Fitz-Gerald's pub, The Hooded Cloak, whose Oak Room served as a festival club, is where musicians went after performing. Those musicians who stayed on after the gig were accessible and enjoyed themselves in the company of locals, joining in pub sessions throughout the town and in the square. As it turned out, many were generous and clearly revelled in performing with other talented musicians.

It was also planned that international stars, organised by the agents, would go off to Cork and Killarney in their chauffeur-driven cars to avoid being mobbed, though it's difficult to believe that the discerning crowds, up close to their music idols, would have done them any harm, or even given them the satisfaction of that kind of adulation. This was Ireland, after all.

Request for Permission to Keep and Use a Still or Stills Without a Licence..

(a) Martin Fitz-Gerald

The Hooded Cloak

Main St. Macroom, Co. Cork

request permission to use without licence the Still(s) specified below.

(1)

PARTICULARS OF STILL(S)

Serial Number or identifying mark	Full content of boiling chamber of each ordinary Still (not working capacity) Gallons	Capacity per hour of Distilling Apparatus Gallons	Material of which constructed	Purpose for which it is to be used.
Nil	40 qts		Tin and copper	Amusement

(2) Address of premises where the still is to be kept. — Main St. Macroom Co. Cork

(3) Situation of the room in which the still is to be used. — The Square, Macroom

(4) Whether it is intended to keep or use Spirits or mixtures thereof at the premises. — Not intended to distill spirits

(5) Whether applicant has been previously authorised to keep a still without licence. — No

I (We) undertake, if permission is granted, that I (We) will permit any Officer of Customs and Excise to visit the above premises and inspect them and the still(s) at any time.

Signature *(b)* John M. Fitz-Gerald

Address *(c)* The Hooded Cloak

Main St. Macroom, Co. Cork

Occupation or business conducted. General Merchant

Ex. No. 3.   No. 667/2004.   Date 18/5 1976

3. Liggers, Legends and The Edge

The 1976 Festival

The first concert in 1976 started with all the basics in place.

To add authenticity and to provide a visual aid to reflect the festival's name, a pot still was placed in the square, manned by distillers known as Batty Joe Canavaun and his cousin Dinny. Sadly no longer with us, their real names were Roger Dealy and Donal Lucey. But their licence was certainly for real when, after protracted negotiations, the legalities were covered. After all, the festival could not be named after anything but the real thing. The licence applied for allowed for the the use of a still, but all that was dispensed was distilled water. It was said that people got drunk on it anyway, such was the atmosphere.

Thursday 17th June 1976, the first day of the first festival, was fraught with excitement and anticipation. Throughout the day a loudhailer announced the day's activities from a car, along with music of the forthcoming performers. The driver even took music requests from the public.

Frank Hall, who at the time presented the RTÉ television programme, *Hall's Pictorial Weekly*, had a wry sense of humour along with an irreverence for politicians. He had no fear of giving voice to anarchy and was a perfect choice to open the festival. He set a relaxed pace, reflective of the fun that was ahead, and the crowds loved him. Former Cork footballer Kevin Jer O'Sullivan also spoke at the opening.

A parade was led by majorettes and the Millstreet Pipe Band, and included community groups and a large float containing precious cargo. Frank Hall entered Cork Street on it, together with the poitín still and its distillers, followed by two donkeys loaded with turf and bottles for the week's work ahead. The parade continued to the square where Chairman of the UDC Seamus Burke welcomed Frank Hall who then lit the still. His witty speech and a fanfare by trumpeter Tom Kenton were followed by the release of pigeons and balloons. A pub singing competition got started and a

Cork Civil Defence Majorettes *Cork Examiner/Evening Echo*

match of local teams was played. The first festival was underway. Concorde had been launched earlier in the year, on 21st January, and at twice the speed of sound, the sonic boom provided far less of a thrill than that of 17th June for Macroom's take-off.

The big bands were popular, but drew nothing like the crowds that gathered for Faithfull. Her association with Mick Jagger, tales of drugs and alcohol and her hit records, drew in numbers beyond expectations. Her frail figure belied a stronger voice, and fans bayed for encores.

Some acts did not attract the anticipated large crowds, and events ran at a loss. The high cost of the rental of The Dome imported from the Rose of Tralee Festival and the expenses needed to fund security and other services were higher than anticipated. Without a bumper night the festival was in trouble and a second festival was unlikely to happen. Marianne Faithfull did the business and ticket sales rocketed.

A vast range of community activities included music competitions for accordion, fiddle, tin whistle, uilleann pipes, sean nós singing, poetry and set dancing. An Lá Gaelach, held that and each year, was important to underline the local culture. Parades went on throughout the week and on Day Four an old time parade revealed local memorabilia, such as equipment for buttermaking used for demonstrations, spinning wheels, penny farthing bicycles and later a fancy dress parade. A flower show, fashion show and strawberry fête followed over the next days, along with a treasure hunt, football matches and a road bowling competition. A pig race, followed by a barbecue, were closely connected, as explained later. A raffle, and finals of the various competitions, were crowned by a sky diving and hot air balloon display, stunt fighting, rock breaking, motor bike jumps, a human ramp and car stunts, to bring eleven days of the first festival to a close.

Seamus Burke UDC with festival directors John O' Callaghan, Anthony Murphy, Denis Murphy, bugler Tom Kenton *John Sheehan*

1976 poster Declan Buckley

RORY GALLAGHER

& BAND plus GUESTS

OPEN AIR CONCERT

IN THE GROUNDS OF MACROOM CASTLE

SUN. 26ᵀᴴ JUNE

2·00 — 7·00 PM.

TICKETS £2·50   IN ADVANCE   FROM

GALWAY	ZHIVAGO RECORDS, U13 SHOPPING CENTRE, HEADFORD ROAD, TEL: 091 64198
LIMERICK	MUSIC STORES, 67/68 WILLIAM STREET, TEL: 061 47703
WATERFORD	MUSIC MAN, BARROW STRAND STREET, TEL: 051 75622
MACROOM	SOUND CENTRE, MAIN STREET, TEL: MACROOM 340
CORK	PAT EGANS, PATRICK STREET TEL: 021 55057
DUBLIN	PAT EGANS, NASSAU STREET TEL: 01 771640
TRALEE	KIELYS, 4 THE MALL, TRALEE, TEL: 066 22951

MACROOM MOUNTAIN DEW FESTIVAL PRESENTS

RORY GALLAGHER

AND HIS BAND

THE CIMARONS

JOE O'DONNELL'S VISION BAND
JENNY HAAN'S LION
HOT GUITARS   STEPASIDE

AND OTHERS

OPEN AIR CONCERT

IN THE GROUNDS OF
MACROOM CASTLE

SAT. 24TH JUNE 2.00 pm

TICKETS £4 IN ADVANCE £5 ON DAY

CASTLEBAR   FITZGERALDS MUSIC CENTRE, MAIN ST.
CORK   TNT RECORDS, 10 PAUL ST.   KILLARNEY   KIELYS RECORDS
DUBLIN   ALL GOLDIN DISC SHOPS   LIMERICK   MUSIC STORES, WILLIAM ST.
GALWAY   ZHIVAGO RECORDS, SHOPPING CENTRE, HEADFORD RD. MACROOM FESTIVAL OFFICE, MAIN ST. PH. 4
                                                      TRALEE   KIELYS, 4 THE MALL.

1977 poster Declan Buckley

Macroom Mountain Dew

FESTIVAL

17 ~ 26 June 1977

Souvenir Programme

The 1977 Festival

Learning from both the success and near failure of the first festival, the committee knew that big names were essential to draw the crowds. Rory Gallagher was targeted and eventually secured as the main attraction for 1977. The potential attendance at his concert had to be catered for, and The Dome was far too small. The GAA pitch in the Castle grounds was surveyed by Rory Gallagher's brother and manager, Dónal, with festival directors Martin Fitz-Gerald and Donal O'Callaghan. The idea of dealing with the enormous amount of sound equipment could have been daunting, but this was the town that had the first electric street lighting in Ireland, and the first mill run on electricity. Back even further, in Neolithic times, a stone discovered outside the town was found to have electromagnetic properties. The town that never reared a fool had energy and would overcome any obstacle.

Pricing the tickets for the Rory Gallagher concert was a conundrum. Costs needed to be covered, but prices needed to be kept low enough for fans. The festival started in a time of economic downturn in Ireland, though recovery was somewhere in sight, and, while it ended when inflation

was pushing up house prices and flat rental, young music lovers had little cash to spare. Amidst the fashion for lava lamps, batiks and bean bags, macramé pot holders and toasted sandwich makers, cars were still rare amongst the young and the less affluent. Many Gallagher fans would have to travel long distances to see their idol and this needed to be considered.

Eventually a price of £2.50 per ticket was agreed – about €20 today. That ticket could instead have bought about six pints of

19

Guinness, or four with a 75p hamburger from McDonalds which opened their Irish first outlet in '76. Captain America's had opened in '71 in Dublin where Chris Davidson (de Burgh) was resident singer. The Shambles on Cork's Paul Street had beaten them to it and opened for burgers, complete with the fancy addition of iceberg lettuce, in 1969.

Rory's concert was expected to attract thousands. And they came. Accounts in this book from the festival directors and other performers underline the work that went into catering for fans who arrived from all over the world. Macroom had never seen the likes of it. There were no Portaloos in those times so a block of lavatories was built, along with security fencing, corrals and whatever it took for crowd control and to make sure everyone paid the agreed entrance fee. Dónal Gallagher's view of the requirements are explained later in the book

The construction of the stage, its surrounding security and backstage areas was an enormous challenge and was taken on by engineers Michael Lynch and Paudie Murphy; Charlie Leonard, a site conveyancer with a building company, and Donal O'Callaghan who supplied pallets from his business PalFab Ltd to create height for the stage. Four 40ft articulated trailers were lifted onto the pallets to support stage flooring and two towers were erected to support the speakers of the sound system The structure was further secured with strong acrow props, normally used in building to prop up structures. Scaffolding with a covering of tarpaulin provided protection for the the sound and lighting system which came from London. Mike Lowe of Britannia Row/Stage Shows, who had worked with Gallagher, agreed with Dónal on what was needed, and that Cork-born sound engineer Joe O'Herlihy was ideal to work it all. A large Rory Gallagher banner stretched across the stage. Dónal, watchful and creative, found a stage backdrop in the Town Hall. It was painted with an image of Macroom Castle – just in case there would be any doubt that this was a Macroom stage! A baby grand piano was hoisted into place and given a final tuning. All was ready.

Committee members : Front, left to right Pat Kelleher, Pat O'Connell, Denis Murphy, Donal O'Callaghan
Back, left to right: Paudie Murphy, Tom Counihan, Michael Lynch, John Martin Fitz-Gerald, Charlie Leonard *John Sheehan*

Numbers arriving at the festival reached 20,000. As hoped, there was a large contingent from Northern Ireland, including a coachload of the 100-strong membership of the Northern Ireland Guitar Society. U2 member The Edge, aged 15, attended, apparently Adam Clayton too, not yet famous enough to be noticed, standing in the crowds without fuss. Legends were there, legends were created.

On the bill with Rory Gallagher were blues guitarist Roland Van Campenhout from Belgium, Nutz from England and local band Sunset. The concert thrilled fans from start to finish, but no matter how good supporting acts were, Gallagher was the reason for their attendance. Just about every interviewee in this book records the excitement of seeing Gallagher as being one of the most memorable moments of their lives. Whatever the amount of effort of all who were involved in this success, it was worth it. Gallagher's performance, with bassist Gerry McAvoy, keyboard player Lou Martin and drummer Rod de'Ath sizzled, zinged, rocked, lifting music into the 'Stratocastersphere'.

There were plenty of liggers – posers and hangers on – who came to be part of the scene, adding colour, or reporting on it. Sometimes disruptive, most were genuinely there for the music. All of them knew they were at a special event.

In 1977 there were plenty of bands who filled The Dome and the Castle grounds before the Gallagher concert. There were nine other days of entertainment. The Cotton Mill Boys (fresh from their appearance on *Opportunity Knocks* and *The Benny Hill Show*) played The Dome midweek, The Bothy Band, Glenn Miller Sound, Reform, Mud, Michael O'Callaghan, The Freshmen, and Tina and The Nevada with Ronnie Medford were back by popular demand. There were plenty of free activities and entertainment from Cork trumpeter Marco Petrassi and his Travelling Dixieland Band, to Murt Kelleher on accordion who gave several recitals over the years of the festival.

Community activities, the competitions, the sporting activities, were added to by a 'bed of nails' exhibition, the hefting by strong men of a 56lb weight over a bar, and rock breaking which appealed to the muscular, while a wall of flame and tunnel of fire added colour. More colour was added with an influx of Hare Krishna members, heads shaved and in robes dyed in vibrant colours, chanting and banging their drums as they walked the streets. They offered free vegetable soup to anyone who wanted it, along with a welcome into the fold. The Samaritans, too, had a caravan. Food could be found for anyone entering the eating competition held on the square. Bread, eggs and cream crackers were on the menu. Hungry bikers purred into town too, adding a bit of black leather to the Bohemian scene.

There were all sorts of demonstrations, including one concerning the capture and transportation of cattle, and another exhibiting sheepdog skills. In that year, £300 was an attractive prize for the coarse fishing competition. Other sports demonstrations included sky diving, stunt fighting, stunt car crashes and Karate. The road bowling tournament echoed the town's tradition in the sport. The events were so successful in the first year that most of them were repeated for all of the festival years ahead.

1977 was Year Two of the festival, though some consider it to be the first as it was the

Frank Hall *Cork Examiner/Evening Echo*

first of the big concerts to be out of doors and the first Rory one. It was a success, not least due to the media attention achieved by the most ridiculous and effective PR gambit: the invitation to Idi Amin to the festival (more about that later). Frank Hall was back to officiate, community activities continued with recitals from Skibbereen Silver Band, the Band of the Southern Command, Dublin 'T' Company, Midleton Brass Band, Fermoy Brass Band, Millstreet Pipe Band and the Butter Exchange Band. There was a car treasure hunt, the Youth Club crazy football match, a history walking tour, a fashion show, a pub quiz, the Youth Club Rag Day, a barrel race, a pint bottle race, an eating competition, a Bridge night and a drag hunt. No shortage of things to do.

Further excitement was added by RTÉ's Mike Murphy's 'burial' by Frank Hall – another event which attracted good media attention. This event is described by Mike Murphy later. Another good boost to the publicity machine was the launch of *Hot Press* magazine at the festival when editor Niall Stokes filled his car with copies of the first edition and generously distributed it.

Cork Examiner/Evening Echo

Macroom
Mountain
Dew

FESTIVAL 1978

16 — 25 JUNE

Souvenir
Programme

The 1978 Festival

Media attention and solidly good music led to a third successful festival in 1978. Bands now wanted to play at the festival, ideally on the same bill as Gallagher, but anywhere at all in the festival programme. It had become a key part of the musical calendar.

Mike Murphy opened the festival this year, along with the release of balloons and pigeons, and the Band of the Southern Command added its usual pomp and ceremony, and a few good tunes. Free events continued throughout the week with Macroom Boy Scouts, Mayfield Majorettes and recitals from brass and pipe bands.

An Ghaeltacht Beo exhibition opened in the town hall and another recital of the Band of the Southern Command, along with the Barrack Street Pipe Band and the Butter Exchange Band and later by the Mayfield Brass Band added to the festive atmosphere. Sporting and cultural activities, successful in the previous years, were repeated and prizes well fought for. In the Church of Ireland a talk entitled 'Make a Long Story Short' by James Cooney was followed by a recital by Comhaltas Ceoltóiri Eireann, and Ceol agus Scéalaíocht o Cúil Aodha at the Palace Cinema. On the Sunday a mass in Irish was sung by Peadar O'Riada's Cór Chúil

25

Aodha. Radio Macroom announced the winners of senior bowling in Masseytown, while Comhaltas Ceoltóirí Éireann gave a recital on Murphy Platform in the Square. There was free entertainment for all.

The first Sunday afternoon of the festival had a family day of entertainment with a garden fête and open-air 'musical jamboree'. This featured Brendan Grace, who introduced short-trousered Bottler to his fans, The Nevada with Ronnie Medford, Jimmy Crowley and Stokers Lodge, Christy Ryan and his music, Finnegan's Wake and Paddy Reilly ('The Town I loved So Well' was his biggest hit to date. 'The Fields of Athenry' was to come later in 1982).

Later in the week, Macroom Races were held in the town park and there was pony trotting and pig racing, a crazy boat race and a display by the Dolphin swimming club, frog racing and turkey racing. A flower show, fashion show, monster fancy dress parade, drag hunt and strawberry fête were held, and the Harp Lager Pub Singing Competition was adjudicated by Sean Ó Siocháin. After the second semi-final of the pub quiz on Thursday 22nd June, the festival barbecue, billed as Ireland's largest, was held at Coolcower House, with music by the Big 4 showband.

There was a children's disco in The

Paddy Reilly *John Sheehan*

26

Brendan Grace *John Sheehan*

Dome on early one evening, and a baby show to involve all ages in the festivities. Many sporting activities continued their success of previous years.

Roly Daniels, Sonny Knowles and Brendan Grace (assisted by roadie Brendan O'Carroll), and Ronnie Medford with The Nevada appeared in The Dome again. One of the highlights of The Dome performances was Limmie and Family Cooking from Alabama. Gimik, fronted by comedian Jon Kenny, sparkled, and fused The Dome lights for a while, and a double bill of Anna McGoldrick and Joe Cuddy kept people on their toes. Nothing like the British dance group Love Machine, though, who got male hormones racing. Accounts of their performances from a few angles appear later. The first commercial supplement with *The Cork Examiner* was produced for the festival and was an impressive publication full of details about the bands and all the activities. It created further interest in the festival.

The festival club in the Oak Room of The Hooded Cloak was a venue for music throughout the seven years of the festival, and typically in 1978 saw music by Tears, Chimes, Kartells, Chips, Dominos and Friends, as well as plenty of impromptu sessions as people relaxed after a long day's work or indulgence in activities.

1978 saw an estimated 17,000 arrive on the day before the return Rory Gallagher concert, 4,000 pitching their tents in fields around the town. More arrived on the day. All guesthouses and hotels once again were fully booked.

In support this year were The Cimarons, the first reggae band to come to Ireland, with Carl Levy on keyboards, Franklyn Dunn on bass, Locksley Giche on drums, Maurice Ellis on drums and Winston Reid on vocals. The performance got the crowd going. With their jumping around the stage, onlookers would have found it hard to resist their infectious joy. When they threw their hats in the air, the crowd saw it as a further excuse to express their abandon and not many stayed sitting on the warm grass. Joe O'Donnell's Vision Band, the first to expose Irish music lovers to the electric violin, showed his virtuosity and he played, sang and danced around the stage with exuberant energy. His album *Gaodhal's Vision* had been played over loudspeakers the previous years, as well as on the radio, so it was a powerful, familiar sound. The former lead singer of Babe Ruth, Jenny Hann aka Janita Haan with her band Lion, was one of the few women to perform at the festival – there were surprisingly few on the circuit. She packed quite a punch. Local bands

Hot Guitars with Joe O'Callaghan out front delivered their usual spirited performance, and Stepaside completed a hearty bill of fare on what came to be called Rory's Day.

While fans enjoyed the support acts, the anticipation of Gallagher was always hanging there, and when he appeared on stage, the Castle grounds came alive. They were not disappointed by a more pared-back, raw style of performance. Gone were drummer Rod De'Ath and keyboard player Lou Martin, replaced by drummer, Scotsman Ted McKenna. Bass player Belfast-born Gerry McAvoy survived the cut. His and McKenna's recollections feature here later. There was no grand piano on stage this year and it wasn't missed by many fans who preferred this older-style Rory. Fans wanted more, got more, and finally Gallagher left the stage happy with a very satisfactory gig.

Hot Press magazine previewed the festival with Rory Gallagher on the cover, with plenty of coverage of the other acts. The *Hot Press Awards* were created and held in Coolcower House, attracting award-winning musicians and hangers-on. They created their own publicity, including a much-indulged John Lydon (Johnny Rotten), there with Bob Geldof and BP Fallon, who knew how to work the media to get column inches.

This was a year that takings were lower than the previous year, due to the public finding inventive ways of getting into the festival grounds free of charge. The security company commissioned from Galway to top up local support was not up to the job. The lessons of Woodstock where they gave up on trying to charge entry, and Glastonbury where ticket control was extremely tight, were well learned here. The year was different to the previous one, but an undeniable success.

29

MACROOM
MOUNTAIN DEW FESTIVAL
JUNE, 16th - 25th 1978

FRIDAY, 16th June –
Opening Parade Led by THE MUPPET SHOW and SIX Bands
Official Opening by –
MIKE MURPHY, R.T.E.
Pub Quiz, Band Recital, £100 Raffle.
Dome Dance
Direct from Sweeden - STARDUST
Festival Club, Oak Club.

SATURDAY, 17th June –
IRISH DAY Competitions all Day
'AN GAELTACT BEO'
Official Opening by Minister of Gaeltact MusicalRecital by Comhaltas
Ceoltoiri Eireann, Historical Lecture, Set Dancing Competition
SENIOR BOWLING Semi-Final
Dome Dance - Roly Daniels Band
Festival Club—Oak Club

SUNDAY, 18th June —
GARDEN FETE
AND OPEN-AIR MUSICAL JAMBOREE
IN CASTLE GROUNDS
Featuring - Brendan Grace—Nevada—Paddy Reilly—Ronnie Medford—
Jimmy Crowley & Stokers Lodge—Chris Ryan—Finnegan's Wake
Football Championship — MILLSTREET v DOHENYS
Band Recital — £100 Raffle
DOME DANCE –
Love Machine & Gimik
Festival Club—Oak Club

MONDAY, 19th June -
Car Treasure Hunt, Children's Disco, Ladies' Football Match,
Glassaley Tournament, Terrier Racing, Pub Quiz, Soap Box Derby,
Classical Musical Recital, Cooking Demonstration, Floral Arrang-
ement, Open Air Ceili and Bonfire Session.

TUESDAY, 20th June -
Youth Club Rag Day, Novelty Items in Streets, Crazy Boat Race,
Canoe Racing, Jazz Session, Senior Bowling Competition Semi-Final
DOME CONCERT at 10.00 p.m. —
SONNY KNOWLES
FESTIVAL BALL - in Coolcower
MUSIC — BIG 4.

WEDNESDAY, 21st June —
MACROOM RACES Town Park – Children's Sports, Folk Mass,
Children's Fancy Dress, Donkey Derby, Pony Trotting, Classical
Music Recital, Pub Quiz, Band Recital, Fashion Show and Cabaret,
Tramps Disco.
DOME DANCE - CHIPS Festival Club
Oak Club

THURSDAY, 22nd June —
MACROOM RACES – Town Park, Children's Disco, Ireland's
International Pig Racing, Newmarket Pipe Band, Classical Musical
Recital, Historical Lecture, Pub Quiz Semi-Final, ¡Monster Bingo
Session¡

Ireland's
Biggest **BARBECUE** Coolcower
House

FRIDAY 23rd June –
SULKEY RACING – Town Park, Children's Disco, Band Recital,
Frog and Turkey Racing, Historical Lecture, Pub-Quiz Final,
£100 RAFFLE
Dome Dance - from U.S.A.
LIMMIE AND BAND
Festival Club—Oak Club

SATURDAY 24th June —
Rock Recital, Speakers Corner, Open Air International Rock Concert -
RORY GALLAGHER
AND BAND
Plus – The Cimarons, Joe G'Donnell's Vision Band,
Jenny Haan's Lion, Hot Guitars, Stepaside.
2 p.m. to 7 p.m. Tickets in Advance
DOME DANCE - REFORM
Castle Ballroom - STEPASIDE Festival Club
Oak Club

SUNDAY 25th June —
4 Ball Golf Competition, Midget Car Racing, Accordion Band
Competition, Baby Show, Band Recital, Adult Fancy Dress,
Final of Glassaley Tournament, £200 RAFFLE
DOME
DANCE - PAPER LACE Festival Club
Oak Club,

PERK'S AMUSEMENTS NIGHTLY
RADIO MACROOM DAILY

GAELTACT BEO EXHIBITION
DAILY TOWN HALL,

Macroom Printing Works

1978 poster Macroom Printing Works

MACROOM MOUNTAIN DEW FESTIVAL PRESENTS

Paul Brady
Jim McCann
the Dubliners
Davy Arthur
and the
Fury Brothers
Paddy Reilly

macroom castle grounds
Sun 17th June
3.00pm
tickets £2-50
from

CORK — URSULA'S RECORD SHOP, OLIVER PLUNKETT STREET   DUBLIN — GOLDEN DISC, DUKE STREET
       KELLY'S RECORD SHOP, GRAND PARADE   GOLDEN DISC, NORTH EARL STREET
KILLARNEY — KIELY'S, NEW STREET   GOLDEN DISC, DUN LAOGHAIRE SHOPPING CENTRE
LIMERICK — MUSIC STORES, WILLIAM STREET   TRALEE — KIELY'S, THE MALL

31

The 1979 Festival

In 1979, a year that saw the Pope visit Ireland, a warm welcome was given to the late comedian/actor Frank Kelly. He opened the festival before Father Ted's Fr Jack Hackett was a twinkle in Graham Linehan or Arthur Matthew's eye.

In addition to showbands and groups, this year's new feature was an Irish folk and traditional open-air concert compered by RTÉ's Donncha Ó Dúlaing. Starring Paul Brady, the late Jim McCann, The Dubliners, The Furey Brothers and Davey Arthur and Foster & Allen, on a blazingly sunny day, it accentuated the Lá Gaelach, which continued since the first year. It was supplemented with many events held throughout the week, including Irish dancing competitions and a culture exhibition.

Tony McCarthy, the Comhaltas member who arranged the competitions, was overwhelmed by the standard of the musicians. There was an historical lecture by James Cooney in Church of Ireland, Sean O'Rahilly-Mahony gave a presentation on Canon Sheehan. There was a session called 'Laugh with the Poets' by An t-Athair Padraig Ó Fiannachta from Maynooth College as well as 'Jokes Are No Laughing Matter', a

Frank Kelly
Cork Examiner/Evening Echo

talk by UCC's Professor Des McHale. Among sporting activities were hang gliding, coarse fishing and football leagues. The evenings in The Dome featured Big Tom and The Travellers, Reform, Memories, and Ireland's Biggest Barbecue was held on 21st June at Coolcower Estate with music by The Circles.

That Saturday, an afternoon of Rock featured Southpaw, Small Change, Sunset, Shampain, White Wine and The West Cork Band. The arrival on Sunday of walkers from Cork to Macroom competed for attention with hot air ballooning, an archery demonstration from the Irish National Archery Federation and more hearty music from the Band of the Southern Command.

That year's festival ended in the Dome where The Mixtures sang their 'Pushbike Song'.

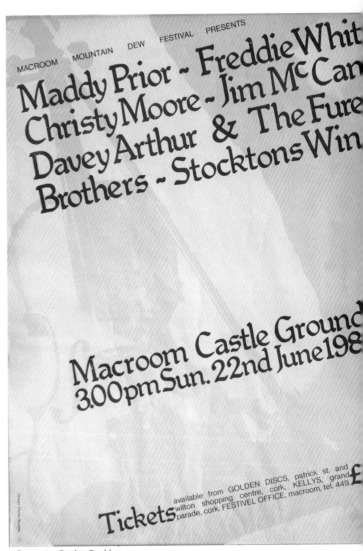

MACROOM MOUNTAIN DEW FESTIVAL PRESENTS

Maddy Prior ~ Freddie Whit
Christy Moore ~ Jim McCan
Davey Arthur & The Fure
Brothers ~ Stocktons Win

Macroom Castle Ground
3.00pm Sun. 22nd June 198

Tickets available from GOLDEN DISCS, patrick st. and wilton shopping centre, cork, KELLYS, grand parade, cork. FESTIVEL OFFICE, macroom, tel. 449. £

1980 poster *Declan Buckley*

1980 poster *Declan Buckley*

The 1980 Festival

1980 was the Van Morrison year and what a masterstroke it was to get him to the festival. London-based booking agents Asgard were commissioned to supply international acts to fill the key dates and this was the first of them.

Morrison had quite a day of mixed fortunes, knocking out a crowned front tooth and having a surprise encounter with someone backstage – more later. He is said to have turned his back on the audience while he tuned his guitar, but diehard fans never mind this as long as his musical performance comes up to scratch, and they report that as usual, it did. Mike Oldfield played his 'Tubular Bells' piece and did not disappoint fans, taking time later side-stage to play on The Chieftain's Paddy Moloney's uilleann pipes. As usual, The Chieftains captivated an attentive audience with their individual blend of instruments, skillfully played: always a happy performance. Lindisfarne's set was rated by many as one of the most memorable of that year's festival.

Maddy Prior, formerly of Steeleye Span, this time with her own band, headlined the open-air concert on the first Sunday of the festival and fans appreciated her acoustic session when the power broke down for a short time. People asked her to put away the microphone when the PA was fixed and continue the set without it, such was their appreciation of her distinctive voice. Christy Moore, The Furey Brothers and Davey Arthur, Stockton's Wing, Jim McCann and Freddie White performed as part of what fans agreed was a particularly good collection of talented performers. The concert was compered by RTÉ's Pat Butler.

Mike Murphy returned to open the festival, and again an impressive collection of bands led a parade to The Square where recitals by Mayfield Majorettes and Boys' Brass Band were followed by the Millstreet Pipe Band, Macroom Accordion Band and Millstreet & Ballingeary Pipe Bands. Daddy Cool and the Lollipops was the first band on stage at The Dome and later Marmalade, the Roly Daniel's Band, Banditz and Margo headlined there.

Perks Funfair continued to provide entertainment all day and night. Community events, successful from previous years, kept going apace, including a senior citizens' get-together and a snooker tournament. A highlight of the week was the ceremony of the twinning of Macroom with the Breton town of Bubry in France which was part of the Festival Ball of that year. This was to lead to a further twinning in 2000 with Marcallo

Cork Examiner/Evening Echo

con Casone in Northern Italy, which today continues as a three-way 'tripling' so that each town hosts the two towns together for a unique event in Macroom every three years. Relationships between the next generation of the families have continued far beyond the festival.

1980 playbill Declan Buckley

MACROOM MOUNTAIN DEW FESTIVAL BY ARRANGEME
WITH ASGARD PRESENT

van morrison

lindisfarne:paul brady
special guests the chieftains
acroom castle grounds: sun. 29th. june

kets available at: **cork:** golden discs shops and ursulas records. **dublin:** golden disc shops **killarney:** kiely's records. **tralee:** kiely's records. **macroom:** festival office, tel 449. **£8**

38

The 1981 Festival

1981 saw some changes to the festival. New committee membersip resulted in a decision to move the larger concerts from the Castle grounds to Coolcower House where the river could act as a natural barrier and where one admission gate was controllable. Community activities continued, though the weather was so warm for the pipe band competition on Sunday 21st, that no-one turned up!

It was a year of mixed fortunes in Ireland with the Stardust fire, Republican hunger strikes in the Maze prison and an inconclusive general election campaign. Music fans of all ages needed a break and Macroom had plenty to offer. The generous bill of fare featured Elvis Costello, some of whose performance was featured by RTÉ on its Summerhouse programme, presented by the late Áine O'Connor with the late Vincent Hanley. The segment showed the enthusiastic thousands that gathered for Costello's concert, and despite some reports of fans needing to be calmed down (a few beer cans did fly past Elvis' ear), it was a performance, as usual, for music lovers and musicians, rather than lovers of standard 'pop' or Rock music. Costello has admitted that this was not a good time

Elvis Costello
Cork Examiner/
Evening Echo

39

in his life, but as usual, he was a pro' and soldiered on. The Blues Band featured well, too, and got the crowd rocking. At one point Paul Jones spotted Paul Brady, listening at the front, and gave him a microphone. 'Maggie's Farm' was quite an anthem for them then, given the times that were in it, and was always a gig singalong number for the audience. Paul Brady led the chorus.

McGuinness's impressive pedigree includes playing with Manfred Mann (he still plays in the band's offshoot, The Manfreds). He was half of McGuinness Flint (who were joined then by Benny Gallagher and Graham Lyle who wrote, amongst others, the hit 'When I'm Dead and Gone'). Hughie Flint played with The Blues Band for many years too, as did other members of the band, returning

Well-established and fronted by Paul Jones, they were dressed in smart jackets (for some of the set, at least) and hit form, winning over the large crowd. Guitarist, bassist, composer and film producer, Tom

to play with their friends. McGuinness, like his Irish seanchaí grandfather, is also a good storyteller – his recollections appear later in this book.

It was perfect timing for British Rock

Claire Hamill *Eddie O'Hare*, Sonny Condell *Cork Examiner*, Feargal Sharkey *Eddie O'Hare*

band Sniff 'n' The Tears who appeared on the same bill. They had just released their *Fickle Heart* album with its single 'Driver's Seat'. Singer-songwriter Paul Roberts gives his account of his experience later. Rocky de Valera and The Rhythm Kings were well in tune with their audience, along with Paul Young and Q-Tips, who captured a young, new audience, even the punks with their

brass section, the sound was fulsome and exciting. Young would later become even more famous.

Scullion followed with the only acoustic set of the concert with Philip King singing, Sonny Condell on guitar and vocals, and Greg Boland on guitar. Masters of their instruments (including their voices), they pleased their fans and acquired new ones,

challenging, spikey hair, still unusual at the time. Young, as usual was particularly popular with many musicians there. With his rasping voice, and the matching tenor and alto sax player Nick Payne leading a strong

with particular appreciation of Sonny Condell's thrumming hit composition 'Down in the City'. The Moondogs performed too, and, unlike his solo appearance in '79, Paul Brady had his five piece band with him. They

Paul Jones and Paul Brady, Paul Young *Cork Examiner*

attracted a big crowd to hear the singles, now classics, from his *Hard Station* LP: 'Crazy Dreams' and 'Busted Loose'. As usual, Brady related well to many fans. Wishbone Ash, heavy and metallic, included backing singer and composer Claire Hamill coming out front to give an energetic performance. She was one of the few female Rock performers at the festival.

The Pretenders did not show up, so The Undertones were promoted to top of the bill on the second day of that weekend. The band attracted a young crowd for this set, who sang every word with Feargal Sharkey of 'My Perfect Cousin' and 'Teenage Kicks' and jumped with the energy of happy rebelliousness.

Musician and composer Shay Healy was in the crowd for that concert. It was a good gathering of, and for, music-lovers.

Rocky de Valera and The Rhythm Kings. Martin 'The Lizard' Meagher (lead guitar), Rocky de Valera (vocals) and 'Shea Stadium' (bass) *John Sheehan*

Phil Lynott *John Sheehan*

The 1982 Festival

In 1982 there was no television celebrity to open the festival. Instead, local Dáil deputies Donal Creed TD, Frank Crowley TD and Tom Meaney TD, along with Seamus Burke, Chairman of Macroom UDC, did the honours, releasing hundreds of balloons and acnowledging the wide range of talented bands which paraded at the opening.

Speakers' Corner, which allowed anyone to have a rant about anything, continued in McDermott Square. Community activities, successful in past years from sporting action to artistic expression, had a sheep race amongst the more unusual. It was the year that the accent was on the word 'community' with a change of emphasis from Mountain Dew and Rock. The format was still much the same. Community activities and events had always been important. Matches were still fought hard, glassy allies clicked, darts landed, bicycles whirred as men and women competed separately, fish were baited, sheep raced. And, on Monday 21st, wood was cut, to be used in the giant bonfire that followed. The smell of pipesmoke added to the woodsmoke, long before the 2004 smoking ban. An open-air céilí finished off the evening. The next night featured the challenge of the slow bicycle races. There was a car driving skills competition held in The Square on Wednesday 23rd with a face painting competition open to adults as well as children. The next night a donkey derby was followed by terrier racing, which had its moment of surprise when the fake motorised rabbit (a miniature car with a piece of cloth over it) was not as fast as one of the terriers who threw it aloft and tore apart the poor imitation, causing a mixture of mirth and shock amongst onlookers.

Macroom Girl Guides held a fashion show which was followed by the usual big barbecue in Coolcower, and the Tadhg Kearney ceilí band provided the music for the Aghinagh Comhaltas ceilí and old time dancing. There was more dancing to The Duskeys and Rosetta Stone, Zen Alligators and Driveshaft who entertained in The Dome.

This was the Phil Lynott's year, with his concert again held in Coolcower. The *Solo in Ireland* version of his *Solo in Soho* tour, was a break from his Thin Lizzy band, except for the keyboard player Darren Wharton. The rest of the band comprised session musicians from his *Philip Lynott* album, along with Robbie Brennan and Jerome Rimson from Detroit who had played bass for the Motown record label (he was living in Ireland then), and was recorded at Windmill Lane Studios in Dublin. All of those who met their mop-haired hero still talk about how warm he was, helpful to other artists and easygoing with fans. Still, it was a gig that didn't attract big crowds, perhaps due to the fact that the band had appeared in a festival in Mullingar a week beforehand. In any case, the mere 1,000 who attended did not get what they hoped for. In spite of the clear billing, they still expected the drive and excitement of Thin Lizzy and

Freddie White *Cork Examiner/Evening Echo*

had little patience with the toning down of one of their favourite Dubs. The support acts went down better with the crowds. Neuro were up first, and the Waterford-based 'new-age music' act played their hearts out. Local band Driveshaft followed and later rocked the crowds in The Dome. They were followed by Belfast-based heavy metal band Sweet Savage who gave as good as they got from a segment of bikers, noisy and aggressive, who arrived to hear Phil Lynott. The Atrix followed and were described by Southern Star journalist Con Downing as delivering a more 'mellow' set which included the late, hugely talented John Borrowman, and also TJM Tutty who had recently replaced Dick Conroy. The Rhythm Kings, back from their successful performance the previous year, did the business again.

Moving Hearts performed their hits 'Hiroshima Nagasaki Russian Roulette' and 'Landlord'. The line- up was stellar, with Davy Spillane on pipes and Keith Donald on saxophone, delivering their distinctive sound collaboration. Donal Lunny on guitar, Christy Moore singing, Declan Sinnott on mandolin, Eoghan O'Neill on bass and Matt Kelleghan on drums discharged their exciting, fulsome sounds in their unique, Celtic musical expression.

DJ Stevie Bolger kept the crowd going between acts.

The next day's line-up was strong, but still attracted a less than satisfactory attendance. Those who did attend were given good value in the shape of The Chieftains, Lindisfarne, Roy Harper, Freddie White, Clannad, French 'psychedelic' Folk/ Rock musician Jean Yves Marie Tourbin, and Salonika. Their concert on Sunday 27th June provided a strong musical finale to the 1982 festival.

It was to be the last concert.

The increased cost of reliable security was one factor in the demise of the festival. While earlier, disciplined organisation by the original committee may have had minor flaws which allowed for a small percentage of freeloaders, the new committee did not replace it with a better system, and, coupled with lower numbers, takings were down. The festival had always paid for extra policing and extra Council services. This included anything from waste bins (not always adequate, if we look back at photographs taken on the streets) to top quality posters – these are now collectors' items, found for sale on eBay. All building services were paid for and no-one was expected to contribute their time and expenses free of charge. Many of the dance bands received a percentage of the takings – some would want 70/30 in their favour, compared to the normal 60/40 split. That did not leave much to pay for the rest of the festival, which had many free events.

The heart of the committee, the board of directors, built up a skillset that took huge energy to sustain. Succession planning may have been weak. Perhaps they had made it all look too easy. New committee members felt it needed a stronger community feel and The Macroom Community Festival name, which once was an add-on to the original Mountain Dew Festival, became the title of the overall festival. In some of the promotional material it was also simply called the Macroom Festival. This may have caused a little confusion and diluted the hard-earned marketing advantage.

It's difficult to pin down all the reasons for the end of an era. Whatever the festival's flaws, the motivation which spurred it into existence in the first place was genuine and in the best possible spirit. If the aim was to bring business to the town, the committee succeeded in that beyond their dreams and expectations. A victim of its own success, The Mountain Dew Festival spawned other festivals and concerts nationwide, and in a time of continued recession, music lovers divided their patronage between them. Energy and enthusiasm – a selfless commitment to do their best – was echoed in the support of the townspeople of Macroom – the Macrompians – who, once they got over their initial fears, allowed people to sleep in their doorways and turned a blind eye to simple pranks and survival tactics. It was all good fun. If it had to end, it was best to quit now.

With playground equipment paid for by the earlier and more financially successful years, the festival managed, at least to some degree, to give something permanent back to the town. If name recognition is one of the most fundamental of marketing tools, the festival succeeded there too. Many who mention the name Macroom at home or abroad, will be asked "Isn't that the place where there was some kind of great Rock festival at one time?"

arr Furey, Pat O'Connell, Donal O'Callaghan, Jim McCann, Donncha Ó'Dúlaing Cork Examiner/Evening Echo

5th MACROOM FESTIVAL

SAT 27 JUNE

ELVIS COSTELLO and THE ATTRACTIONS

• SNIFF 'N' THE TEARS

• MOONDOGS

• RHYTHM KINGS

plus special guests

THE BLUES BAND

SUN 28 JUNE

THE UNDERTONES

• PAUL BRADY & HIS BAND

• Q-TIPS

• SCULLION

plus special guests

WISHBONE ASH

booked by Asgard

D.J. DAVE FANNING
gates open at 11.00, music starts at 12.00
tickets £8.00 for Sat., £7.00 for Sun. or £12.00 for the weekend

1981 poster Unknown designer

JUNE 26th   **Saturday**

★ PHILIP LYNOTT ★

★ MOVING HEARTS	SWEET SAVAGE ★
★ ATRIX	DRIVE SHAFT ★
★ RHYTHM KINGS	NEURO ★

★ D.J. STEVIE BOLGER ★

6th MACROOM FESTIVAL

JUNE 27th   **Sunday**

★ LINDISFARNE ★

★ CHIEFTIANS	CLANNAD ★
★ ROY HARPER	JEANYEVS TOURBIN ★
★ FREDDIE WHITE	SALONIKA ★

Tickets: Sat. £8—Sun. £8—Weekend £13

Gates open at 12.00 midday
Music starts at 1.00 p.m.

Full Camping and Catering
Facilities Available

John Sheehan

4. From the Horse's Mouth

Nobody knows the real story of the festival better than the ambitious (and a little wild, perhaps) directors and committee members who got the whole unlikely event off the ground. I asked them how, why and when they got involved, and, as well as they could, to recall the excitement, sense of fun, and tense moments, during those heady days.

Cork Examiner/Evening Echo

52

Ted Cotter
Festival Director

" I was treasurer for a few years and as a primary teacher found myself involved in a lot of the activities with young people. I wasn't very free, as the primary school term was still in progress, and I was working in Cork while living in Macroom. I remember that we all worked extremely hard during the festival time. We were young and hearty and more than capable of overcoming any difficulty that arose. We put on feiseanna on Saturdays when there was no school, and our Lá Gaelach was important in bringing people from the outlying villages and towns. I worked with Assumpta Ní Chasadaigh for the Irish dancing competitions as she was Secretary of the local Chomhaltas. Mrs O'Sullivan, who had a dancing school, helped out too, as well as Murt Kelleher, a local musician.

We rented out the Castle Ballroom, the Bishop McEgan Vocational School and upstairs in the Town Hall for the various stages of the competitions. Dancing would go on from 9am to 6pm. We organised children's art competitions, too. When you involve youngsters, whole families come with them. It was all made easier when Údarás na Gaeltachta came on board. I'd like to think the festival was multicultural, which meant we needed to showcase home-produced talent too. We were located just outside the Gaeltacht, so it was good to see helpers coming from within it to Macroom. Harnessing what you can from the community was part of the ethos of the festival.

The pig races were run on the main street up towards Main Square. It brought in people from the hinterland. We were trying to be different, to have original ideas to attract people. The community-themed weekend provided varied activities for everyone, and they had such a happy time they would say that they would come back again. That was music to our ears. I didn't have a lot of time to go to concerts, but I enjoyed what little I saw. If a problem arose you would be called away, so it was 100% giving, and we all lived on a couple of hours' sleep, sometimes none. I had to be bright and early for school on a Monday, so that wasn't so easy.

I saw the two Rory concerts, the first one being the first open-air concert in Ireland. Even famous concert promoters hadn't come up with that idea! It was fabulous to showcase our Rory. He drew thousands. The first concert for me was more exciting, a trip into the unknown. We did whatever it took to make it right. It was a revolutionary moment and something to be proud of. I can say I am glad to have been part of it, and I missed it when it ended.

Those of us on the original board of directors became great friends. We grew up together, but became stronger, firmer friends during the festival. There is a Rory Gallagher celebration every year, Cork Rocks for Rory, when a tribute band gets us all together, often in the outside area of TP Cotter's pub. It's usually on a Sunday in June. I have been at the last three. We sit down and enjoy a more intimate open-air concert and think back to the festival time.

John Sheehan

Tom Counihan
Festival Director

" I was working for International Tapes in Macroom and I wasn't part of any club, more friends with members of the Junior Chamber.

Frank Hall was a huge draw and people loved him. He stayed with Anthony Murphy's family in Poulanargid, where he obviously felt at home.

The AIB bank did something it had never done before: opened on a Sunday. This was to facilitate our transaction for Van Morrison. Bands from outside Ireland were often paid in dollars. Van's manager came with a committee member to get the dollar draft for him. We were glad the bank was open so we could deposit the day's takings.

Tim Cooper Kelleher, a psychiatric nurse, was Van's driver of the day. He also looked after the festival horse races in the town.

I was Chairman for two years and my main job was with the electrical side of operations for many of the concerts. The output at the Gallagher gig was amazing to see being set up and to hear. Fire officers came to each gig a few hours beforehand to do a check, but I don't remember any trouble.

About 15 record shops countrywide sold tickets, taking 5% commission. The posters were designed here in Macroom by graphic designer Declan Buckley (now a garden designer based in London) and printed in the UK. The agents of the bands insisted we had the posters well designed and printed. I went over to the UK to pick some of them up and was charged a fortune in duty to bring them in through the airport.

For me, apart from Rory, obviously, one of the best bands was Lindisfarne.

In 1981 the big concerts were moved from the Castle grounds to Coolcower to try to take control of the crowds and stop the number of people intending to sneak in without paying. To save money on delivery of the big tent, Fitzie and I collected it from Ballisodare. It was like two circus tents joined up, with the performance area covered and some of the public area open.

Coolcower worked well for us the first year when you came in only through the main gates, with the River Lee on one side serving as a natural border. For the second year, people found ways of getting in free. We had cut back on security a bit to save money which was not a good idea. My lesson learned from the festival over the years is to keep the committee small. Once it gets big, people try to offload duties. It's better to keep it tight. "

Cork Examiner/Evening Echo

55

Maurice Cullen
Festival Director

❝ I was hired as Head of Security for the first Rory Gallagher concert, and returned to that post for the majority of the following festivals. At the time I was with International Paper Sacks. I had a black belt in martial arts so was moderately equipped for the job, and recruited Judo club colleagues such as Teddy Leahy, another black belt. We also drafted army personnel from the Fermoy Barracks.

With the river on one side, the Castle and golf club on the other, the area could be moderately secured. It was the hill open to the road that presented the problem. I had around 80 diligent people manning the venues and we used lines of scaffolding to filter the crowds. We couldn't allow bottles through as there were a lot of kids playing in the venue. Broken glass would have been problematic. For me, safety of the grounds was even more important than security.

One young man swam the river with his clothing in a bag and was met by security and given a whiskey to warm himself up. Soon after he was told to get dressed and put on extra padding for when his backside

would be kicked!

I had to close down one food seller who was using a side entrance of a shop to sell food. I was worried about hygiene, and safety was our priority. We had a responsibility to people. Marjorie Corcoran (who later became my wife) was Chairman of the UDC in 1977. She publicly gave out about businesses boarding up their premises for the first Rory concert. She was perturbed that all businesses didn't get into the spirit of the festival. The fear passed and everyone eventually relaxed.

There were no mobile phones then so we used walkie-talkies, but they were noisy and we had to go on top of a roof to get reception, so they were more for show! We checked people on the way into the town and got them to leave their rucksacks, tent poles etc in The Dome with security guards in attendance. We were being over-cautious, but we couldn't take any chances. They were able to go into the Castle grounds concert venue free of their gear, which suited them too. While the weekends were the busiest, we had to be vigilant every day of the week, with volunteers picking up bottles in the street. I had lived in Dublin so I had a darker perspective on how awful these events could get.

I remember that Van Morrison banged his head off the scaffolding, having already been given a clatter of a can in King's Hall Belfast earlier that weekend. Not a good weekend for him. Lindisfarne were terrific, getting numerous calls for encores. Paul Young was a tiny little fellow with a huge band and his soul music was brilliant. The Cimarons were great craic, their curly mops a pantomime. "We are The Cimarons", they shouted and everyone cheered. The Blues Band was fantastic too. I enjoyed them all.

I liked being backstage in the thick of it, meeting everyone, while at the same time watching out for their safety. I thought I was very trendy with my ponytail and leather jacket!

I'm not ashamed to admit that I hadn't a clue how to run a festival, but I got guidance from Martin Fitz-Gerald in all matters! I got a great kick when I saw The Edge on a documentary called *Ghost Blues,* mentioning the festival as the first open-air Rock concert in Ireland and the influence it had on him.

Rory Gallagher arriving with Gerry McAvoy, Dónal Gallagher, Rod de'Ath, with Civil Defence member Michael Hallissey
John Sheehan

Majella Elliot
Ladies' Committee

" I worked in the bank and was one of three women on the committee who was not married to a member of the board of directors. I think Martin Fitz-Gerald was keen to effect some kind of gender balance! It was top heavy with men, alright. I think Martin got more than he bargained for, as we were independent, single women with plenty of opinions about how things should be done. We had always had a good relationship with him, as we used to borrow gear from him for the pantomimes.

Three of us organised a fashion show which was kind of posh at the time. That went well. I also remember sitting in the little caravan which was a real crock, taking money for The Dome dances. We sold a lot more tickets than we expected. We were almost throwing money on the floor, it was coming in so fast.

Another memory is of Rory Gallagher, who had been taken to the golf club to change. Someone on stage announced him, but he wasn't there! He hadn't been brought into the GAA pitch. It caused some delay but it was fine in the end. I wasn't so in awe of Rory as his family banked where I worked in Bridge Street in Cork. I knew all the family. Nobody thought the festival would be such a great success. For the first of the Rory concerts in 1977, we baked queen cakes and scones and gave them out as young people arrived looking very tired, having walked or hitched from Cork. It may have been a culture shock for the town, but the crowds that came in for the festival were all lovely.

I was in Coolcower for the Hot Press Awards and thought people like Johnny Rotten were spaced. We were innocent and they looked very different – all punky. It was all major excitement for us and we enjoyed it all. "

Cork Examiner/Evening Echo

John Martin Fitz-Gerald
Festival Director

" All we were trying to do was to promote Macroom. We were wondering how to bring people into the town. We had little capacity for accommodation, relative to the expected needs, so we organised camping in a few locations. We had a good relationship with the Gardaí. There were older guards who were very sensible. If anyone was causing trouble they didn't bother with arresting them. Instead they would drop them six miles out the road and let them walk back in to cool them down. We got some minor negative publicity at the time, but what would happen is that anyone the drugs squad wanted to catch in Cork, would be watched for in Macroom, and they would arrest them there. There was more dope smoked on the streets of Macroom at other times than during the festival.

I had a pub called The Hooded Cloak and by law I had to keep it closed on Sundays until after the last mass. This day during the festival, I got a knock on the door and it was the Gardaí telling me that they needed me to open ahead of time because the Corpus Christi procession was on its way and a few hundred men were congregating at the cross with nowhere to go. I obliged.

We were using a car-mounted loudhailer to promote a band named Crúibín & Harp who were performing at The Dome as support for Horslips. The band's real name was Inchiquin, but we asked them to change it for the duration of the festival. We thought it would generate some publicity. We were on a tight budget so any scheme we could think up to draw attention to the festival was tried. Harp was a well-known draught lager in Ireland at the time and the brewers were corporately sponsoring the Harp Lager Pub Singing Competition at the festival. On cue, a Garda came up to me, referring to the invented name and told me we had no licence to sell Harp beer in The Dome. He had no problem with serving crúibíns! When the publicity idea was explained, he took the joke well. We didn't get much publicity out of it, but it caught the imagination of the public reading the programme.

Another promotion, this time paid for by us, was bringing out the first ever commercial supplement with *The Cork Examiner*. The supplement was rolled separately and not folded into the newspaper, and consequently most of them got separated and were not distributed with all of the newspapers. As a result, the supplements today are folded within the newspaper for everyone to enjoy.

I didn't get to many concerts, but I

remember Maddy Prior. At one point the sound system failed. She calmly took her guitar and sat at the front of the stage and sang acoustically. People loved her and appreciated the voice they recognised, particularly from 'All Around My Hat', her hit song with Steeleye Span. So much so, that when the power came back on and she returned to the microphone, people shouted to her to get rid of it and get back to singing without it. She really won the crowd over.

I remember the Band of the Southern Command playing the National Anthem before one of the football matches. They had played at various venues throughout the festival, but that day immediately packed up and went home. They weren't allowed to play other pieces after the National Anthem. That was the convention, so there was no more music from them after that.

I particularly enjoyed the speakers' corner. Located just off McDermott Square, it gave everyone an opportunity to rant or speak about anything they wanted to. Hundreds would gather to listen. You'd learn a lot about what was on people's minds!

I was also impressed by Archdeacon Denis O'Connor who prayed the weather would stay fine for the Rory Gallagher concert. Another first for Macroom!

We had lots of publicity ideas mentioned later by others in this book. Some worked, some didn't, but they were all worth a try.

I enjoyed the festival while it lasted. I could see that we had set a pace for other open-air concerts which sprang up around the country – Dalymount, Lisdoonvarna, Athlone, Salthill, Sligo. As well as that, once the festival became successful, agents and managers got involved. Artists' fees shot up which in turn pushed up ticket prices. The festival committee was lucky to be left with 10% of ticket prices which, on the profitable years, went to creating a playground. We twinned Macroom with Bubry in Brittany, France in 1980 and later with Marcallo con Casone in Northern Italy. These happy associations were spearheaded by the festival and we have enjoyed the benefits ever since. And we put Macroom on the map.

Cork Examiner/Evening Echo

Mary Fitzgerald
Ladies' Committee

" I have a few vivid, but not very long, memories of the festival. One was of taking money in the caravan next to The Dome. It was such a wet night I think people were getting in just for shelter. The money was coming in thick and fast.

Another is when we had a family fun day in the grounds of the Castle. I was elected to be a fortune-teller, so I dressed up in lots of scarves and a long dress and read palms. I knew nothing about fortune telling and no-one was under any illusion that I did, so we had good fun. It was a wonderfully sunny day and there were great crowds around, an awful lot of parents with children. People of all ages.

I went to the Hot Press awards in Coolcower House and I must admit I was totally dumbstruck by Rory Gallagher. I know he was a shy kind of person, but he said 'hello' to us and smiled and I felt like I was the only person there. I was unable to speak! I can't tell you who else was there as it seemed like the awards were just about Rory. I didn't care about anyone else.

My greatest highlight was to be side-stage at his concert. That was a perk of working on the committee. We didn't get any green blazers like the men on the committee, but this was better for me. I could see an ocean of people out front and I wondered what it was like to be him looking at all those people in front of him, there, just for him. It was an extraordinary moment. To have this amazing concert on our doorstep was hard to believe. And it's hard to believe it's forty years ago. These days I'm lucky to be working in the Rory Gallagher Music Library of Cork City Library. "

Pat Kelleher
Festival Director

I was in charge of looking after the celebs during the festival. Not a bad job to have. I minded the people who were backstage, providing them with drinks – the hangers-on too, and there were plenty of them! I remember looking after Mike Murphy who was MC one year.

I was secretary of the committee from the start until 1980/81, and we really didn't know what we were taking on. But our committee meetings were properly done. We had minutes and everyone was kept informed about what they needed to do and what was going on. That, and a lot of youthful enthusiasm, got us there.

We were in our early twenties and thirties and stone mad. When a few groups first got together such as the Junior Chamber of Commerce, GAA and the Youth Club, no one group was prepared to take on the festival so we formed a strong committee of people who worked well together. We wanted it to be a music festival, but also a festival that had entertainment for all the family. It was by pure chance that we managed to get Marianne Faithfull to give us our great start in 1976. We booked her through her agent and we apparently just hit at a good time. My late wife Bernadette loved her music so it was a particular thrill for us. After her performance she joined us in the Oak Room, where this photograph was taken with Bernadette. We had a lot of fun. She was lovely to deal with. To me she was the star of the seven years of the festival. She was a huge draw for our first year. Macroom was jointed with her fans.

I was surprised at how much I was impressed by Rory Gallagher. His wasn't my kind of music, but he was a terrific performer and won me over. He brought in a huge crowd.

For me the years of the festival were all absorbing and my business on the main street, located just off McDermott Square where I sold TVs, records and tapes, became a minor distraction.

It's hard to credit how we managed it all. There were obstacles, but we seemed to overcome them. We were winging it, but we had some fun! Not a day passes that we don't talk about it.

Courtesy Pat Kelleher

62

Charlie Leonard
Festival Director

"My main job was to look after the staging. I had graduated as a structural engineer the year before, and worked with Sisks Builders.

The committee had little money or equipment so we had to do the best we could. We were young and probably foolish enough to take it on. There were no units like they have these days so we had to start from scratch. We constructed toilets on the campsites and set up chemical toilets in the Castle grounds. We rented The Dome from Tralee but we had to erect it. It was all part of a unique open-air experience.

We had to deal with infrastructure to allow for the pig races, horseracing and other numerous activities, often setting them up and taking them down before the next event. We set up a corral at the Castle gates. We also had to be sure that people such as Rory Gallagher wouldn't be mobbed by fans. We brought him on site via a farm road from the Black Gate side. He was the most unique artist.

Marianne Faithfull's was a stand-out performance for me. She was not brash, more soft, and she absolutely held people's attention. They came to see who was this woman who had a liaison with Mick Jagger, and she was fresh in everyone's memory from her 'Dreamin' My Dreams' hit the year before. There were thousands of people going through The Dome. We were letting them in one door and they were going out the other side. It was a huge event. My memories are coloured by my youth at the time, rose-tinted glasses perhaps, but it was a fantastic night."

MACROOM MOUNTAIN DEW FESTIVAL
RORY GALLAGHER
OPEN AIR CONCERT
SUNDAY, 26th JUNE 2 - 7p. m
GROUNDS PASS

ISSUED TO : ....

ISSUED BY : ....

Margaret Linehan
Ladies' Committee

" My uncle Tim Cooper Kelleher was very involved in the festival so I joined in as a youngster selling ice-cream at the gigs. We also had a tea and sandwiches stall where we charged very little for everything as we could see the young people were starving. I lived near the bull sculpture at the entrance to the town and we would feed tea and cakes to the young people as they passed. A lot of them had walked from Cork and looked exhausted.

The crowds were amazing, good humoured and polite, so much so that we let then set up camp in the field beside our house. I can't vouch for the hygiene standards! Those of us working on the committee got in free to the concerts. I would have done anything as I was dying to hear the music. Friends from Cork and the surrounding area of the town came and stayed, sharing our beds. Without a doubt it was the biggest thing to ever hit " Macroom.

Eleanor Lynch
Sales

" I was on duty for the years of the festival in the caravan just inside the Castle gates where we sold tickets. Many people had already bought tickets before they got to Macroom, and others tried to get in free, but still there were plenty who hadn't. We were very busy all the time. There was a bit of pushing and shoving to get to the top of the queue, but there was always pleasant banter. I was too busy to get to the concerts, but the caravan was only 100 yards away from the stage so we could hear everything.

I was more interested in dancing at night to the bands in The Dome. That was more my kind of music. When the festival was over, I was given enough money to buy an electric lawnmower which I had " always wanted!

Michael Lynch
Festival Director

" I was the stage designer of the festival and a team of us constructed the Rory Gallagher stage. It was quite a task to complete in the time allotted to us. Apart from that I can remember on one concert day, a Sunday, wading through the throng with a bag containing a pile of notes. A lot of money. I was taking it to the bank which had accommodated the committee by allowing for an instalment to be made over the counter on the weekend. It would be made against a banker's cheque which was to be paid to Van Morrison. It was a slightly nervous walk. The festival really put the town on the map; it was successful but there's a life span for everything. "

Cork Examiner/Evening Echo

Anthony Murphy
Festival Director

❝❝ When people from the Junior Chamber and the youth club came together they were genuinely interested in addressing the problem that Martin Fitz-Gerald described in no uncertain terms as 'the town being on its knees'. We were determined to do something for Macroom. When a Rock festival was a possibility, a bottle of brandy which we shared one night after hours in The Hooded Cloak, cemented the idea.

Strangely, even the next day it still seemed like a good idea. Martin had experience with bands for his pub/nightclub and other members also booked bands for youth club and various community events, so it wasn't all that difficult to take the first steps. When Martin, Denis Murphy and Matt Murphy were prepared to underwrite the costs, we were able to put the wheels in motion and the festival got started. Over the years some people were convinced that we were all making a fortune, which wasn't the case. There were huge expenses, even for acts that didn't draw big crowds.

My function was to get publicity and deal with managers once the bookings had been made through agents. People like Jim Aiken, the Hand brothers – Jim and Michael – were tough to deal with initially, but they were okay as time went on. There was always talk about the position their acts would have on the programme, and of course what they would charge. When the smaller bands got to hear they would be on with Rory Gallagher, they tried to up the price. We argued that it was an honour for them to be anywhere near him on the bill.

Coolcower House was a great asset to us, and Evelyn and Timmy Casey made a great team and coped well with all the performers who stayed in their private setting away from everyone. The Hot Press awards were held there too.

I believe that the Cork Jazz Festival got their idea from us, as some of the celebrities who flew in to play at the festival stayed in the Metropole Hotel. It wasn't only businesses in Macroom that benefitted from the festival. People stayed in Killarney and points between Macroom and Cork.

The Dubliners were very entertaining and would play sessions in the pubs afterwards, often in The Hooded Cloak. People came into Macroom from other parishes and went to their own favourite pubs that they would use as changing rooms for matches. There were no fancy dressing rooms in those days.

I remember The Cimarons arrived on a private plane. I was there to greet them as, playing the bongos, they danced into Arrivals. They were quite a sight with their high, striped, knitted hats enclosing their dreadlocks. The band had organised a mini-bus for themselves. People enjoyed their performance which was nothing like anything we had seen before. I like that kind of music, with its different beat and energy.

I had to deal with the backlash of the Idi Amin brainwave which was purely devised to bring attention to the festival. And there was quite a backlash. Once we got the idea of inviting him in 1977, we decided there was no time to waste. Late in the night, John O'Callaghan drafted a letter and Pat Kelleher went home for his typewriter and typed it up while the rest of us stayed on to read and tweak it. We delivered a copy to *The Evening Echo* within hours, at the same time as posting the original to Uganda. The paper picked up on it and wrote a story that appeared the next day.

We wrote to the Ugandan President, inviting him to attend the festival. We never expected him to come, of course. We ended up having interviews all over the world and with all the Irish media who picked up on the Echo article. Mission accomplished! I contacted Frank Hall who came to open the festival. He was a huge success due to the popularity of Hall's Pictorial Weekly.

Frank stayed with me in my family's house in Poulanargid and loved to mingle and chat with the locals. We stopped in the Metropole Hotel in Cork for something to eat before he got on the train back to Dublin and he talked about how successful the festival was. He was amazed that a group of people could get it together and get it so right.

I remember getting to The Hooded Cloak around midnight at the time that Mike Murphy was part of another publicity ploy – his 'burial'. He was due to be dug up from underground in the coffin where he had been buried for three hours. This was located in the field behind the pub. Mike had gone underground during daylight and it was pitch dark when he was exhumed. It all went well and afterwards Mike and I went for a few pints to different pubs to celebrate his resurrection. Denis James's (Murray's) pub was one of them and when asked to do his famous 'dance' he obliged and amused the customers. We went back to the festival club for more entertainment where a great night was had by all.

I still have my green blazer that we had made for all the directors of the festival. We thought we made a smart team and could take on anything. And we enjoyed every minute.

Breda Murphy
Spar supermarket Macroom

" My husband Denis was very involved with the festival from the start. He was Chairman of the Board of Directors. He died at a young age when our youngest child was four. We had five children, one born in 1969 and four of them during the festival years, so I didn't get to all of the concerts. While Denis was out on festival duties I was minding our Spar supermarket. We have always lived over it. During the festival late at night we had a hatch to serve people minerals, chocolate, crisps and so on. People came into town with their sleeping bags and we had no worries about them when they were sleeping in doorways. I remember that they opened The Dome at night after the performances and let people in to sleep in their sleeping bags. They had security on duty and there was no trouble, and it was useful to help cope with the crowds arriving in the town. There was a campsite out of town too.

I got to some of the concerts and thought Rory Gallagher was excellent. I still have my ticket stub for Phil Lynott. I'd meet the girls, the wives of the committee members and the other members of the ladies' committee, in the evenings in the Oak Room Festival Club in The Hooded Cloak.

I remember the lads bringing Frank Hall home here for spare ribs. The committee would come here and cook sausages in the middle of the night. They seemed to like the thick sausages I had in the fridge!

I remember lovely nights at the Festival Ball. It was a black tie affair, so we all dressed up and enjoyed a bit of glamour away from the day-to-day workings of the festival. There was always a big crowd at it.

My sister Phil Barry and friend Ann Counihan sold the tickets at the Marianne Faithfull concert. Their kiosk was a window in a tiny caravan in the front of The Dome. They got a bit anxious as the queues were very long and people were so impatient and keen to get in that they rocked the light caravan in frustration. The committee came to the rescue, but that was the mood of the evening. The numbers were really amazing.

The pubs were very busy during the festival. I remember hearing about two girls who couldn't get into any pub as they were so full. They got the 9.30pm bus to Coolcower House and had a drink there instead! I remember festival t-shirts too and Perks funfair was a great asset. It was a lot of work for Denis, but he enjoyed it. "

Lots of good memories.

Seamus Burke, Macroom UDC; Pat O'Connell Festival Committee;
Chris Reynolds, Area Sales Manager, Beamish & Crawford; Denis Murphy, Festival Committee,
Joe Nolan, Beamish & Crawford; John O'Callaghan, Festival Committee *John Sheehan*

Matt Murphy
Festival Director

" I lived in the town square and had my home above the pharmacy. On the morning of the first Rory Gallagher concert I looked out of the window at an ocean of denim, washing up against the Kanturk Dairy truck as it arrived, filled with milk. This is how many of the fans were keeping themselves alive: the 1977 alternative to bottled water. I ran a photography competition at the time and Kevin O'Brien, who would later become a local teacher, won it with a shot he entitled 'Blue in the Queue', featuring a view similar to the one I'd seen from my window.

Marianne Faithfull provided one of the great nights held in The Dome in the old mart field where Lidl is now. It was completely and utterly jammed. You wouldn't get away with that these days! People were mainly local and from Cork county. The place was buzzing in anticipation of her visit.

The success of the first festival demonstrated to us the need for a more pro-active approach to getting people aware of Macroom more widely as an important place to visit. We saw the significance of drawing people from the centres of population – mainly Cork and Dublin. Confidence came from breaking even on the 1976 festival. I remember looking at Horslips, whose LPs were hugely sought after, performing and thinking to myself, "this is a very big deal."

The festival was a lot of work as we had no mobile phones then, so I seemed to spend a lot of my time running up and down the street, delivering messages.

The second year of the festival was Rory Gallagher's first and we had to add a lot of security measures. There was a lot of pressure as a huge number of people wanted to be there and we were just learning as we went along how to deal with crowds of this kind. I didn't board up my business and nothing happened to my windows. Just a few were nervous about potential trouble. It was really a few years after that that we had any trouble with drugs, and, relative to the numbers, there was very little.

We were concerned about security after the first few festivals as later on it attracted a different element from outside Macroom, which was not good for the town. This was probably a main reason to call it a day after 1982 when numbers were down anyway. The GAA pitch in the Castle grounds was ideal for the festival, but unfortunately it was hard to police. People wanted to get in for nothing and went through the river and ran down the hill, so it was quite dangerous. As time went on, the Macroom people who were not used to this kind of behaviour started to avoid the festival. The committee got fed up of it, as much of it was voluntary work, and it started to become less enjoyable. With numbers down in 1982, we made a decision. Denis Murphy, Martin Fitz-Gerald and I were the underwriters, so with the rest of the committee we decided to call it a day for the festival. I didn't lose money, only perhaps a little on the last year. Some performers were very decent when they could see we had problems. I won't forget the generosity of The Chieftains.

People still remember the festival, and even young people here take a pride in the fact that this town managed this achievement. "

If I stood at the top of Mount Massey
What a wonderful sight I would see.
I'd see all its hills and its valleys,
Including Sullane and the Lee.

Old poem

John Sheehan

Paudie Murphy
Festival Director

❝ I helped build the stages for the duration of the festivals. It took about 10 days beforehand and during the festival to get it sorted and to make the best of our resources without paying for too many services. We had to beg and steal, at least borrow, from our businesses, and use whatever skills we had ourselves. We felt responsible to those who had bankrolled the events, so we kept expenses down as much as possible.

The Dome stage wasn't a big deal as a floor came with it. In 1977 we had to construct the toilets and enclosure around the stage along with the corrals for people to queue as they entered the Castle grounds. We couldn't build the corrals too early, just the night before or morning of it, as we needed access through the Castle arch the rest of the time. The challenge was the stage for the first Rory Gallagher concert. We had to build an enclosure around it, and I remember we built the stage starting with pallets, and later when everything was in place, when I was under the stage I could hear the pallets creaking. We really hadn't realised the extent of the load there would be from all the equipment. When Rory's team arrived, they supplemented our work

and knew what they needed. We had to have a canopy too, to keep Rory and the band dry in case it rained. My worry was that if a gust of wind got underneath it could have lifted the whole thing off. These days these things are prefabricated and properly designed. We just threw ours up and hoped for the best.

The sound system for Rory Gallagher's concert was extraordinary. It wasn't noisy, and had a beautifully clean sound.

'Brave' is the word that springs to mind. We were young and fear didn't enter into it. We had nothing to lose. We got a good lot of fun out of it. Madcap fun! If we had thought too much about it, we would never have done it. We enjoyed what we were about. We had a lot more to do other than the staging, as we had all sorts of local activities during the week, such as pig-racing. That all had to be managed to keep everyone safe.

Our meetings a few times a week would be followed by a few pints in Fitzie's. There was good camaraderie. I can safely say that what I learned about business during the festival was better than the four years I did in UCC. It was a nice break from being a civil engineer the rest of the year.

My music interests were centred around Bob Dylan and Leonard Cohen and I was less into Rory Gallagher and more into

Lindisfarne and The Cimarons. Marianne Faithfull was fantastic and seemed to take to the Macroom people. I enjoyed the Love Machine, who were like a latter day Spice Girls, a bit provocative. When they arrived, they were a bit shocked that the changing rooms were so primitive, so it took a bit of encouragement to get them on the stage, but they did. I was impressed with Julie Felix. I wouldn't otherwise have had the opportunity to see a Californian sing live.

You would see hundreds hitching from the Cork County Hall – not something you would see today. It would have been too difficult to gauge how to manage private bus hire to get people to us, and in any case people probably wouldn't be able to afford or want to pay for that either in addition to the cost of the concerts. But they got there in their droves.

Gerry McEvoy, Rory Gallagher *Cork Examiner/Evening Echo*

Brendan O'Brien
Committee member

"I was a member of the organising committee, and as a teacher and headmaster of a school in the town, I was recruited as the person who spoke Irish. I was rolled out when the Minister for the Gaeltacht, Denis Gallagher, came to launch our Lá Gaelach. We paid due homage to him. I was young at the time and it was wonderful to be with him.

My main function was to sort out accommodation for the visitors who came to attend the festival. The musicians generally sorted out their own, so at least they were not my problem. I had an added complication in 1977 when the Rás Tailteann cycle race included the stages Castleisland to Macroom and Macroom to Clonmel. It wasn't just the cyclists; they had a lot of followers looking for beds. It caused quite a whirlwind of activity. They ended up in Ballincollig, Inchigeela and Ballyvourney.

Conscious of the depression of the time, all of us on the committee felt we were performing a social and economic function.

Cork Examiner/Evening Echo

B&Bs were popular, and they did well. The ancillary events all week long added to the social functioning of the town.

Of course, as a teacher, I was keeping an eye on the younger people, as I felt a responsibility towards that age group. There was some apprehension about whether we could control and manage the crowds, and we had to understand and cater for that apprehension. It worked very well and we had very few issues. There was great liaison between the committee and the Gardaí, with loads of back-up. I remember the sea of denim in the town which was tidal. It came in and went out.

I got married in 1976, the year of the first festival, and was building a house. A huge number of personnel was required all over the town and in Coolcower, which had to be secured. We had a team of people standing at walls. I was one of those and was paid to do it, like most people who worked at the festival. I was glad of the income at that time. It wasn't just hoteliers who benefitted from the festival, it was cleaners, the security team, and a lot more, as they all had to be paid.

Along with the engineering team from the festival, I worked on the Police concert in Leixlip, for which we were commissioned to build the stage, on the back of our success

with the Rory Gallagher stage. U2 was the support act. I remember Colman Cotter who was working with us saying that Bono was an effin' lunatic as he was climbing up the scaffolding on the side of the stage which was part of the construction. Our construction! Our stage! I was a labourer and we had taken a week to build it. It was very enjoyable and the Police were nice to work with. The owner of Leixlip Castle, Desmond Guinness, at the time was married to his first wife Mariga (the former Lithuanian Princess Marie Gabrielle of Urach). Their son Patrick would come with his father to watch what we were up to. We got a great sense of importance being part of it all.

On the day of the concert we were not allowed backstage, even though we had built it, and I felt like telling them all not to go up on our stage. We were ushered into another area which was very much the tradesmen's compound. Our inflated sense of worth was soon pricked.

I often wonder if we shot ourselves in the foot by constructing this stage which showed others how to do it, sending music fans away from our own festival. We were flattered to have been asked and didn't think ahead. I'm not sure, even if we had looked that far ahead, that we could have resisted.

Donal O'Callaghan
Festival Director

"We were a bunch of ambitious, adventurous young people with some skills, but none relating to a music festival. From the start there was incredible camaraderie. I was involved with the youth club, along with my brother John, and these young people and those from the GAA made a huge contribution to the festival. They were fantastic, manning gates, cleaning up after concerts, keeping everything flowing well. We often started at 10am and kept going until 5am when it was necessary. A quick kip and we were up again.

We had a lot of community activities. One was a great barbecue and dance at Coolcower House. Each year a pig would be cooked properly in Lynch's bakery for safety, and then finished off on the barbecue.

There were pig races, too. Rasher Dasher was one of the pigs Johnny Warren decided to enter in the pig race, and he really wanted to win. He did a deal with a farmer to get a free-range young pig and share the winnings. For the race the pigs were let off at Railway View and the first through the Castle gates would be the winner. Johnny came up with some kind of concoction to give his pig – the first incident of doping in sport I came across. Rasher Dasher took off like a bolt out of the heavens and straight through the gates, while the others were rooting around on the starting line. He won, but we found him legs up in the air, dead. The farmer got his share of the prize money and we barbecued the winner in Coolcower.

As I helped to build the stages, I was usually watching from behind them, both in The Dome and the Castle grounds. I had a good vantage point for the audience and the performers. Paul Brady was a gentleman to deal with. We had contact with Denis Desmond who brought in Horslips and other bands. I remember that he was wearing sunglasses, even though it was foggy. We thought he was very cool.

Love Machine came from the West End of London and thought they were coming to an international festival, but ended up in a tent with green carpet for a floor. There was a bit of resistance to this difference and their management was threatening to pull out. Eventually they agreed to perform. I was on the stage, and people were heaving with the excitement of this racy performance of girls dancing. At one stage I could see the bright, white collar of a priest in the distance. He was making his way towards the stage and I was sure he was going to stop the performance. The church was still powerful in those days. When he got up close, he put

his hand up to his collar. "This is it," I said to myself "there's going to be trouble", but instead he ripped off the collar and got into the groove, dancing freely to the girls and the music!

There were plenty of serious issues to be addressed. How we would build a stage for Rory Gallagher was one of the biggest. Paudie Murphy, Charlie Leonard, Michael Lynch and I had to solve the conundrum. Four 40ft articulated trailers had to be lifted onto wooden pallets, layered onto each other for height, so we would have a massive stage. It was a crazy thing to do. And then we had to put two towers on the stage for the sound system. We also had to lift a baby grand piano on stage with a forklift. Afterwards a man with a briefcase came along and took out his tuning fork.

Next, we needed a covering in case it rained. We used heavy black plastic. We got tarpaulins from Tadhg Cronin in Crookstown. One tarpaulin we used had the B&I Ferries logo on it. The Monday after the concert the phone rang in Tadhg's office with a complaint about using the B&I logo. We effectively argued that they got a lot of publicity in return for it appearing on the front page of The Irish Times.

The other big issue was the sound system. Only one person in Ireland was up to

it and that was Corkman, Joe O'Herlihy. He was recruited by Dónal Gallagher who sorted out that side of operations. Joe arrived with his wife Marian, both of them lovely. "Do you realise this is the highest sound decibel that has ever been heard in Ireland?" he said. The day before the concert we did a sound check and the clarity was phenomenal.

Rory led the way in thinking big. That seemed to be his point. He arrived in a Jensen Interceptor, a fashionable car at the time. For his second gig the band was smaller, but everything was planned to the last detail. The band this time was back to a more raw Rory. He was electric!

Van Morrison had the misfortune to be at the mercy of a man backstage just before he was due to go on. There had been a problem just before that, as somehow he came through the wrong entrance to the Castle grounds. We had to cut a slit in the black plastic barrier and get him through it to backstage. A large man, perhaps a hanger-on with one of the other groups and definitely not from Macroom, was caught short and was relieving himself. When we suddenly arrived, he turned around in the middle of it and sprayed all over Van, who was livid, of course. I was highly embarrassed, though I wasn't responsible for it, but I will never forget the bad feeling.

We had a caravan close by and Van went into it. We were sure he wouldn't come out. But whatever he did, he came out looking clean and went straight onto the stage without any greeting, performed and went away straight after. This is the truth, and when people say he was in bad form, which they seem to do quite often about Van's other performances, this is one contributory factor to this particular one. He was very professional to have performed at all and we appreciated that. "

Cork Examiner/Evening Echo

John O'Callaghan
Festival Director

" I had just got my degree (a B. Comm), so I had time to give to the committee as secretary for the first festival and in the years following, before I went to work in Dublin in 1980.

As a committee we worked well together. The business people made their contribution, sometimes just very welcome financial support. Others, who were members of Junior Chamber, gave much more. The youth clubs tend to underestimate their influence on the success of the festival. They were a very dynamic group at the time. There wasn't much money around, but they had great fun.

We were young, in our twenties, dreamers and looking for a good time. And it was fantastic fun. We wanted some traditional, family entertainment as well as being a Rock festival, and it seemed to work. We had run weekly dances in the youth clubs so we had a structure of going through agents for bands. Martin Fitz-Gerald also had run events in The Hooded Cloak. We had to up the scale a bit and deal with the magnitude of a big festival.

Looking back, I remember our first meeting which was held in a lean-to of the youth club with a galvanised roof on a grey November night. The Macroom town traders had called a meeting and invited all the associations and clubs to attend. The agenda was to discuss what we could do for Macroom to give trade a boost in the summer. There was a lot of talking, but not much came of it. There seemed to be no fresh thinking, so another group formed out of it and in the end this became the committee, an entity which comprised enthusiasts who were prepared to run with an idea. We formed a limited company and made sure we had a tidy business operation. After that the work started, and the festival took off.

I remember when we tried the Idi Amin publicity gimmick, Fitzie throwing stones at my bedroom window to wake me up, shouting, "Get up! We have an international news story to manage! We are on the front pages of all the dailies, and radio stations are queuing up from around the world looking for interviews." Foreign news agencies picked up on the story. We could expect an interview request from anywhere, at any time. One that I particularly enjoyed was an interview that Martin Fitz-Gerald and I did with a radio station in Sydney. I can still recall the gist of the presenter's lead-in remarks: "... and now we must take a commercial, but stay tuned to your radios. Coming up, we have Martin Fitz-Gerald and John O'Callaghan on the line from Ireland with a bizarre tale of illicit whiskey, a megalomaniacal dictator and a blues guitar superstar." During the interview, when pressed as to why we invited Amin, we played our trump card which was a phrase we decided to include in our letter: "Because great events deserve the grace of great people". It worked every time. Such was the power of the Amin invitation that, nearly 40 years later, it still resonates with complete strangers of that age whenever the Mountain Dew Festival is mentioned.

After the first burst of media attention, there was a lot of speculation about if and when Amin would arrive. As there was an international conference on in the UK at the time, it wasn't outside the bounds of possibility. The media were in the airport just in case. Of all my memories of the Mountain Dew era, the Amin episode is my fondest. It taught me some valuable lessons in media management.

I have a recollection of another brainwave we had when we tried to get the giant costume from the King Kong film which had been re-released in the 70s. We would put it up on one side of the Castle gates with an image of Rory Gallagher on the other. We decided to phone the film producer, a Mr Carli, whom we found out could be reached at his home. This had to be done through the Macroom Millstreet telephone exchange and they were able to listen in. I was told that we would have to get back to Mr Carli in two weeks' time, after his holiday. However, we were under pressure so I decided it was worth trying a few days earlier. When I asked to be put through to his home in Beverly Hills, the telephone operator said to me, "I thought he was gone on holidays!" King Kong didn't make it to Macroom, but Rory's larger-than-life image was used and can now be seen in TP Cotter's pub.

Cork Examiner/Evening Echo

Pat O'Connell
Festival Director

" I was involved in Junior Chamber and was in on the festival from the start, acting as treasurer in the first year. I was just 25 and had an import-export freight business based in Cork Airport. I had a telex machine and this was the means of communication to contact acts around the world. We knew we had to get big names to attract crowds from outside Macroom. I got a phonecall one day, "Send a telex to Nashville and see if Johnny Cash is available!" He couldn't make it, but it was typical of what would happen. We made phone calls or sent telexes as there were no mobile phones or emails. We booked Irish and some British acts through their agents and we were very lucky to get Marianne Faithfull.

We lost money when the Nevada showband played a great gig for about 30 minutes, but there was an ESB outage. We used an extension lead to a building to keep us going, but people had stopped coming in the door when they heard no music. It was fixed too late to be of use. The night of Marianne Faithfull's gig it was my job to move the takings into a safe place as we took in the cash. She was being paid £800 and 60% of the takings. Her manager was

watching everything and counting people as they came in, but we all lost count when the huge crowds arrived. The cashier was in a caravan, selling the tickets and was sitting on a seat with storage underneath and the money went straight into it. It was a huge amount of money. We made money that year and the next, and put the money into equipment for the children's playground.

I remember walking the streets in 1977, the year of the first Rory Gallagher concert, seeing the streets full of people lying around. I said to Fitzie "If anything goes wrong, we'll have to get out of town!" As it

Pat O'Connell speaks at festival opening *John Sheehan*

happened the visitors all behaved well. They were obviously there for the music and had arrived early enough to settle in before the big day. My house was on Railway View in the centre of town. One morning my wife was at the door and saw a man with a rucksack and no shoes. He said he had lost them the night before. She went inside and got some really old brown leather sandals belonging to my father and gave them to him. It was all good fun. People were only drinking pints; there was no madness from shots and they didn't have much money anyway, so couldn't afford all that much drink over the weekend.

I used to play in a band and my father bought me an electric guitar, a red one, from this lady in Macroom which, it turned out, was Rory Gallagher's first electric guitar. I gave it back to him when he came to Macroom. It's probably worth a fortune now.

The Dubliners and The Furey Brothers and Davey Arthur were very generous. On the night of their concert they jammed with others afterwards in The Hooded Cloak. Anything could happen at the festival. Then on the Monday we had a bonfire in the town and two of The Dubliners, Luke Kelly and I think it was Barney McKenna, did a free gig for us at it. In fact, they didn't go back to Dublin for the week and only then to play at their gig at the National Stadium.

The kick I got out of the festival was putting the programme together and pulling it off. It was savage hard work. We would start the next festival a month after the last one ended, but I have no regrets about that. We went to London to the annual dinner of the London Macrompian Association, and as a result some of them used the festival as an excuse to get home, and we were glad to welcome them. John P Quinlan was Chairman of the London branch of the Macroom Mountain Dew Festival and in 1977 he held a dinner which was attended by the Macroom-based committee and had a huge attendance from London which resulted in more Macroom people coming to the festival that year. The festival is part of our history. We were ahead of our time and we were a great team and worked very well together. We got great craic out of it.

Gabrielle O'Leary
Ladies' Committee

" I think I was working in the dry cleaners in those days – there wasn't too much extra business during the festival. I helped organise the fashion show with Majella Elliot and Mary Fitzgerald which was a big thing for us. I remember that Gay Girl Boutique supplied clothes and it's great that forty years later they are still in business. We used local women to model the clothes. I think we also ran the Mother and Child and Bonny Baby competitions. What I do remember is that we had a lot of meetings in the evenings in Fitz's over 'coffee'.

We got passes to the concerts so I went to a lot of them. Rory was the highlight for me, with Marianne Faithfull next. We would go late into the night in the festival club for romance, drinks, craic, big sing-songs with Charlie Leonard on guitar. It was a lot of fun, not all about drink, more of a 'session'. The majority of us were single at that stage, with no notion of marriage – we had to sow our wild oats! "

Cork Examiner/Evening Echo

5. Musicians, Muses and Mischief-making

The memories of performers have been fascinating to collect from interviews done via Skype, telephone, and email.

Sadly, Rory Gallagher left us in 1995 and Phil Lynott in 1986, and many more since then. Other performers struggled to recall the finer details of their time in Macroom. After all, for them it was just another gig, or another booze-fuelled blur. And how many of us can recall what exactly we were doing 40 years ago? There were no mobile phones to wave over a crowd, no iPads, no Instagram accounts, just simple cameras, which people didn't tend to use while they were enjoying themselves. It was a time of 'Mindfulness' before the term was invented. Living in the Now. Enjoying the moment.

But I am grateful to those who did remember – however much or little – and, after some prompting, recalled some wonderful and bizarre moments in the heart of the Cork countryside.

Rory Gallagher Cork Examiner/Evening Echo

Don Hall on Frank Hall

1976

"I confess to being a compulsive hoarder. I hardly throw anything away. It was only when I began sorting through my late father's possessions that I discovered from whom I had inherited this dreadful affliction.

My dad was the journalist and broadcaster Frank Hall. Over his lifetime, he amassed a huge amount. Aside from the obvious effects, he left behind a mountain of newspaper articles, scripts, letters and suchlike from his time in Independent newspapers and RTÉ.

Amongst the many items I came across was a souvenir programme from the first Macroom Mountain Dew Festival held from 17th–26th June 1977 when he performed the official opening.

Organised by the late Denis Murphy and his festival committee, the Macroom event is remembered as Ireland's first big outdoor Summer Rock festival – forerunner to Electric Picnic, Castlepalooza and others.

Described by Denis as 'the most progressive and ambitious in the country', the programme paints a picture of how forward thinking he and his committee were. His fellow directors were Pat O'Connell, John O'Callaghan, John Martin Fitz-Gerald, Tony Murphy, Donal O'Callaghan, Tom Counihan, Matt Murphy, Ted Cotter, Pat Kelleher and Michael Lynch.

Together, they attracted such headline acts as Rory Gallagher, Mud, Glenn Miller Sound, Joe Cuddy, Freshmen, Cotton Mill Boys and others, including Van Morrison and Phil Lynott.

Attractions arranged to entertain audiences during the 10-day long event also featured a number of family-friendly attractions, one of which, at least, would never be allowed in this era of Health and Safety.

The particular event took place immediately following the official opening – at 8.45pm on Day One. Then, according to the programme entry, a certain Mike Murphy, (he, I since discovered, being the Mike Murphy of RTÉ fame) was (and I quote) "to be buried alive 9ft under by Frank Hall in a standard size coffin". Later, at 12 midnight, the programme went on to say what they termed 'the resurrection of Mike Murphy' was to take place.

It's true that Mike Murphy got up to all sorts of tricks as his television career advanced. However, little would one have known that being buried alive for three-and-a-quarter hours was one of them. Indeed, how the Macroom committee talked him

Frank Hall with Batty and Dinny *Cork Examiner/Evening Echo*

89

into performing that little trick is anyone's guess.

On the day before the 1977 Macroom Mountain Dew Festival began, Ireland voted in a General Election that swept Jack Lynch and his Fianna Fáil party back to power.

Next day, as pundits the length and breadth of Ireland were counting votes, it is to be imagined that the people of Macroom were counting how long Mike Murphy would remain underground, and would he still be alive when they dug him up.

As his subsequent rise to prominence proved, he was. As for Frank Hall, according to festival director Pat O'Connell, "he opened the event and he closed it again, having stayed in Macroom for the full 10 days in between."

Sonny Condell

Supply, Demand & Curve 1978;
Scullion 1981

"As Supply, Demand and Curve, we were taking our album *Camouflage* on the road and we were glad to get the gig supporting Rory Gallagher in 1978. We were on quite early in the afternoon, well before him. We could see Dónal Gallagher organising everything. Unfortunately, I was unhappy with the gig. I felt it hadn't succeeded, despite having with me the talents of Fran Breen on drums, the late Jolyon Jackson on piano and cello, Greg Boland on guitar, Brian Masterson on bass with Rosemarie Taylor singing.

I remember lying in the field afterwards watching Rory playing on the back of a truck and being quite taken by him. I think of it as one of those shows you never forget. The weather was nice too. In 1981 I was still playing (as I am today with Leo O'Kelly) as Tír na nÓg, but for the festival I was back as part of Scullion with Philip King and Greg Boland. That was a busy, exciting time for us. I remember watching Paul Young who was fantastic with his big band Q-Tips."

Sonny Condell Cork Examiner/Evening Echo

Cathal Dunne

1976

" I remember the festival well. The people running it treated us all equally. I was just a kid of nineteen, but I loved that I was given such respect, which I was also given later when I was involved in the Eurovision Song Contest, but this was particularly encouraging at the time. The festival was huge for me, though we were quite a small act compared to others. I had been to festivals in Tokyo with my own songs and never won anything, but this one, being just a small part of Dermot O'Brien's show – he was a big star at the time – was a big moment for me. I now live in Pittsburg with my American wife and am still writing songs and performing. I've just finished a book *Put Yer Rosary Beads Away, Ma.* "

Van Morrison's drummer Peter Van Hook with Paul Brady *Cork Examiner/Evening Echo*

Bob Seward

1976

Mountain Dew Big Band

" For the festival I put together a band of 15 top musicians such as Jack Brierley, Tommy Power, Pat Sullivan, Chris Costello and Dave Owens. We rehearsed for a few weeks in Cork and had arrangements of a wide range of music, including James Last tunes. We played in quite a few places during the festival, often going from one gig to another. One night we had a big crowd in The Dome. At that time Fitzy had four bars and we played in all of them. I remember sleeping on benches in them. We all kept running on the high of excitement. That was the year Marianne Faithfull performed and she was marvellous. I met her afterwards in the Skellig hotel and she talked about how much she enjoyed it and what a different experience it was for her. The festival just shows what can be done when you have the drive of local people pulling together. "

Sal Tivy Perks

1976 – 1982, Perks Fun Fair

"" The Mountain Dew Festival was a huge thing for us. We had never before seen the likes of Rory Gallagher who was world class. The town was abuzz, apart from those who were nervous about the arrival of the Rock crowds. The concerts brought in crowds from sixteen year-olds to those in their sixties which suited us as we boast that we entertain people, aged 1 to 101! We do quite a lot of festivals of one kind or another and what stood out about this one was the superb committee. They all seemed to know what they were doing, and what everyone else was – you often go to places and one hand doesn't know what the other is up to – so it made life easy for us. Before we ever got to the festival Martin Fitz-Gerald's late wife Margaret got extra staff for us – we took on fourteen or fifteen local helpers.

We had to do shifts as we usually opened at 11am and went on until two or three in the morning. She was the person I went to if I needed anything. That's not to take away from Breda Murphy, Denis's wife who, with Denis and Martin (known to us as Rocky), comprised the team that looked after us very well. Our site was close to The Hooded Cloak which was also close to Fitz-Gerald's Funeral Home. If a funeral was taking place, Martin would warn us and we would shut off the music until the families had left. There was no problem with that. I can remember a funeral approaching the Funfair on one occasion and there was Martin, walking quite a bit in front of the hearse, limousine and cars, wearing his top hat. He put a finger to his lips by way of confirming the need for a respectful silence while the motorcade rolled past.

The Mike Murphy burial was done on our site so I witnessed it all. It also brought even more business as people came along for the burial and stayed to be part of the Funfair. We were packed! In fact, I wondered if Mike was going to be forgotten!

The committee was very creative in what it came up with to entertain people: I remember the pig race. Even those market stalls that were outside the Castle grounds were innovative for the time. It was clear that the committee had studied the form of festivals abroad and incorporated some ideas. You didn't have to run a mile to see acts. I was impressed with the policing – not just by the Gardaí – there was no 'carry-on'! It was a terrific success, not just for us, but for everyone who made their contribution to it, and of course for the town. ""

Eamon Carr
1976 & 1978, Horslips

" I don't remember much about our performance in 1976. However, I recall flying from London for the festival in '78 to collect a *Hot Press* award on behalf of Horslips. That was a memorable event. I shared a hotel room with Bob (Geldof) and drove around the locality (in, I think, a Mini) with John Lydon (Johnny Rotten), his partner Nora and BP Fallon. We had a lot of fun that weekend.

The Cimarons, a reggae band from England, played that afternoon. They delighted in giving it large with their rap Irie in an Ireland which had the same sense of linguistic discovery, and most visiting reggae acts enjoyed that. Whenever they would invoke the spirit of "Jah!", sections of the audience responded enthusiastically. More than a few thought they were calling out "jar", which they took to be an endorsement of our drink culture.

Later, at one stage, the DJ at the function in the hotel (Coolcower House) allowed me to take over on his decks and I recall playing some of Elvis Presley's early Sun recordings, possibly 'That's Alright Mama', 'Mystery Train' or 'Good Rockin' Tonight'. John Lydon and I later had a discussion on the merits of the great reggae artist Linval Thompson. He had great musical taste.

Amongst others, Rory received an award from *Hot Press* that afternoon/evening. All in all, it was a slightly wild weekend and the chronology remains a bit of a blur. As it should be. But it was a hoot. And the hospitality and courtesy we received was first rate. "

The Edge
1977 & 1978

" I was about 15 at the time when myself and my brother went to the 1977 Mountain Dew Festival in Macroom. We got a package ticket including the coach trip down and back. It was my first time going to a gig. All the best musicians were playing that day with Rory Gallagher. He was an incredible influence on me as a guitar player, particularly early on. I got to know him a little bit and did call him my friend, which was an amazing thing. Rory's legacy will obviously live on in his music, even more than that, in hundreds of Rock 'n' Roll bands, including my own band, which started as a result of his example, and what he achieved with Taste and as a solo artist. "

Road Bowling Cork Examiner/Evening Echo

Gerry McAvoy

1977 & 1978, Rory Gallagher Band

" I live in France now, and my first concert with Rory Gallagher was in the Olympia in Paris in 1971. I played with him for twenty years until four years before he died.

I remember well the Macroom Mountain Dew Festival as we played it twice. I recall the theatre backdrop of the Castle and quite an unusual stage set up on top of wooden pallets. It was quite different, but rural in a good way, in the nicer sense. I remember Hot Press being launched there and the following year that their awards were presented – one to Rory. I do remember Johnny Rotten making some distasteful remarks, but Rory got over them.

At both concerts there seemed to be a connection between the audience and Rory. The atmosphere was great. The band was cooking! Each concert was unique with different musicians except for Rory and myself. For the second one it was drummer Ted McKenna's first time playing with the band, so it was a bit edgy! In fact Rory was quite nervous and when it came to the time of introducing the band, as he always did, I could see that he had forgotten Ted's name, so I called it out. When it came to my introduction, I shouted out 'Gerry McAvoy', just in case! Rory and I were always in synch'.

I could always tell what he would play before he played it and vice versa. It was an unusual telepathy. A romance that worked great. We never had a set list, so we never knew what we would be playing until Rory called it. We often started with a different song. That was no problem to any of us.

I always found it a bit frustrating that it was so rare to have Rock music on RTÉ radio, unlike in the US at that time. It didn't make sense that the festival wasn't covered by RTÉ. The simple fact that it was Ireland's first open-air Rock concert held outside a big city should have been enough to make some kind of news. And they didn't even come to the second one! They obviously didn't see it as important – that was a disappointment, though we were used to it.

The time around the Macroom festivals was Rory's high point in his career. He was on the crest of a wave then. We played in Cork City Hall many times and of course in the UK and in Northern Ireland from where a lot of the fans came for the Mountain Dew. He had a lot of fans in Germany too and it was covered by that German documentary you can see on YouTube. They were ahead in recognising his talent. Rory is a terrible loss to us all and it's great to hear people like The Edge say how inspired by him he was. These days I play in a band called Band of Friends with Ted McKenna from the Rory days and Marcel Scherpenzeel on vocals and guitar in Gallagher style. It's not a tribute band, more a celebration one. We play Rory's style of music, but we all write and slip our own music in, increasingly more. We gig a lot in France and at various festivals around the world and are currently recording a fresh CD. 🙶

Rory Gallagher, Gerry McAvoy *Herman Kemp*

Keith Mulholland

1977, Nutz

"We arrived to a town packed with people lying around, having a laugh. We got to our hotel and we must have looked pretty awful after the journey on the ferry from the UK, as the hotel demanded all sorts of ID before they let us have our rooms. It didn't matter, the sun was shining and that continued to the next day for our gig before Rory Gallagher.

I play drums and sing, and the Mountain Dew was one of a number of concerts we did with Rory Gallagher. We always got on well with him – he was a bloody nice guy – and amongst others, I played a great concert with him in the Palais des Sports in Paris. I remember one time that the sound system failed and Rory just picked up his mandolin and played acoustically until it was fixed. Nothing seemed to faze him. He expected the set-ups to be right, and then he was able to get on with his own job. Rory played a blinding gig in Macroom. He connected with the crowds and they loved him. Today I spotted a poster of that gig on eBay.

The gig was fabulous. The crowds were spot-on. They knew us and our music, so it went very well for us. It was a perfect auditorium – the shape of it – the sound was great. As a result of that gig we returned to Ireland a lot. Hot Press gave us lots of good write-ups which helped. We'd often gig in Belfast and travel over the border – the Troubles were full blown then – and we would be searched thoroughly. We did some gigs in the Arcadia ballroom in Cork. The last one we did there, the deal we had was to share the profits, and a huge number turned up. We did well out of that one.

I still play with a few bands based in Liverpool."

The people running it treated us all equally. I was just a kid of nineteen, but I loved that I was given such respect.

Cathal Dunne, 1976

Gerry Madigan

1977, Cotton Mill Boys

"1976 and '77 were the best years of the Cotton Mill Boys. We had won *Opportunity Knocks* and been on *The Benny Hill Show* by the time we got to Macroom, so we were on the crest of a wave, flying high. We knew Cork already as Pat Coughlan had a ballroom in Fermoy and the Hilton Hotel in Cork, and during our 15 years on the road we often played there. He is one of two people who paid us more that we agreed when the night went well. A rarity! I thought it very enterprising of the town to take this festival on, and it was a unique experience at the time. I remember a day of perfect sunshine when we played at the festival. There was a fabulous party atmosphere.

I missed playing the banjo and guitar and singing, especially when I went to the bluegrass festival in Hillspring, Alberta. My fingers were itching, but I had sold all my instruments in favour of running my business and only had an acoustic guitar. My son Julian bought me a banjo for my birthday so I got back playing and have written and recorded some songs. I used to do record production in Dublin, so I do most of it myself. I hope to be back gigging in Ireland when the album is finished."

99

Jimmy Crowley
1978, Stoker's Lodge

"I can't remember too much, it was more Rock 'n' Roll than folkie, but they did feature folk acts.

We had just recorded *The Banks of Sullane*, so we knocked a bit of fun out of it."

Dónal Gallagher

1977 & 1978

" A lot of effort went into my brother Rory's gig at Macroom, particularly before the first one in 1977. We were anxious that the price of entry would be kept down so his fans would be able to afford to travel from Belfast, Dublin and all over the country. Also, we were very conscious of costs, given the state of the economy at the time, and the fact that many of his fans were students. At the time of Macroom, from spending so much time in Belfast, Rory was aware how the 'border' was perceived from both sides. If I remember correctly, a ticket concession was given to Northern fans who had hired buses in the North to travel and attend his concert. For many Northern fans this would have been their first venture South, to cross the divide and interact with others. To that end it was important to have a space with a larger capacity than The Dome.

I went to Macroom and had a look around with Martin Fitz-Gerald and we explored the idea of putting a stage in the Castle grounds. The space was big enough to take 10,000 fans which we reckoned was a likely number to attend. The grounds had a natural amphitheatre, with the river bordering it for security, so a free-for-all was not on. The gig, with all its production, had to pay for itself, and that meant getting decent ticket sales.

After I got back to Rory with the information for the event, he remained uncertain, as my brother was a little hesitant about doing gigs outside cities in Ireland. It was more costly to put on a concert in Macroom than in London, where all the gear was accessible. Rory had played in large venues and open-air festivals around the world, and at home he would do a run of nights at Cork City Hall.

Contact was made through our mother's house phone initially. I asked her if they called back to put whoever it was in touch with our London office. However, our mother's father's family came from Ballyvourney and they said that I should call the committee back and go down to see them. It's not that Rory didn't want to perform in Macroom, he just wanted the concert to work out for everyone. There had been much talk about others wanting to do an open-air Rock festival back then – it was everybody's ambition to be the first to do it.

Members of the committee and I had intense discussions about the ticket price and our requirements, and £2.50 was agreed on. We would also need to hire in a top quality sound and lighting system. To that end I engaged Mike Lowe of Britannia Row/Stage

Shows, who had worked with us, on sound and lighting, on our tours. He and his team did top concerts with Pink Floyd, Emerson, Lake & Palmer etc. We were very happy with how we worked together out of doors. Mike and I are still friends, and one time at Paul Simon's open-air concert in Kilkenny, we were standing, listening to the music and he said: "And to think this all happened because of Macroom!"

We had approached concert promoter Jim Aiken to run the 1977 event, but he decided not to take it on, so we did it ourselves. It was more work for us, but we were resourceful. We were also experienced at making stages look good and we were glad to have a painted theatre backdrop of Macroom Castle which we discovered in the town hall.

In the days leading up to the construction of the open-air site and stage, I had Joe Herlihy, who was one of our crew, stay and oversee much of this for us. Joe now works with U2. As we put maximum effort into the stage production which set such a high standard, U2's The Edge, only fifteen years of age at the time, remembers being impressed.

We were very aware that Rory's gig should not be a security worry for Macroom, so we consulted with the Gardaí

well in advance to avoid giving the press a field day. The committee paid for extra staff to be on duty, and before the 1977 festival even started, they managed to apprehend some journalists who had brought models to swim naked in the river for a sensational 'Sunday' photograph. They were just looking for stories to take away from the music aspect of the concert, and there was huge exaggeration of violent weapons and drug taking too.

Ironically, the day the British Queen was in Cork, I bumped into the Lord Mayor, his councillors and their head of security for the Royal visit, who said to me "The first security job I ever got was for the Rory concert at Macroom."

Having taken the decision to go ahead with the concert in Macroom, we then had to think about publicity. There was a small budget so we took ads in the UK *Melody Maker* which was read widely in Ireland as well as in Europe. *The Cork Examiner* and *Spotlight* magazine may have been disappointed, but we needed to reach the Northern Ireland audience too.

I was aware that writer Niall Stokes was endeavoring to launch a new music magazine, so I made contact so see if we could launch both around the same time. We found common ground, so effectively *Hot*

Press hit the streets weeks before the 1977 concert, featuring Rory on the front page. The new publication had a great impact throughout Ireland and the UK. It gave us a good boost, and with it we felt some degree of smugness that we were pulling off a big concert outside the main cities.

We lived in Ghent for a while as it was a good gateway to Europe. We enjoyed that city as we were friends with Flemish musician Roland Van Campenhout, whom we would take on tour with us. Given Roland's musicianship and love of the blues, we asked him to come with us for the 1977 Mountain Dew Festival, and we were joined by Nutz from England and Sunset from Cork.

Rory always had stage fright and was worried no-one would turn up for the festival. There weren't all that many advance sales in those days to indicate how it would go. However, he was thrilled with the concert. Rory felt it worked musically, and agreed to do the following year too.

By the end of '77 my brother and his band had located to San Francisco to record an album. After several months he wasn't satisfied with the results and binned it. In the process Rory changed the line-up of his band, though it took much longer than we expected to find the drummer he wanted. Bringing Ted McKenna to start recording drums for 'new' material on Rory's long-delayed album meant that we were only weeks away from the '78 concert and Ted had to learn the full stage repertoire. Rory had wanted more time to prepare for the Macroom gig, but appreciated there was a limited window for the open-air concert. They were rehearsing up to the last minute – they even had a rehearsal in the backstage 'clubhouse' before hitting the stage. It was more than nerve wrecking!

We used much the same sound set up as we had for the first year. However, we had to add more lighting for the German film company which was making a documentary on Rory, as they came to film the Macroom experience too. That meant extra generators, and the stage was improved as well. Following his 'historic' appearance at the Rockpalast (WDR Television), playing live to some 50 million viewers of the Eurovision network, Rory had become a household name in Germany.

In 1978 Denis Desmond (now of MCD Productions) was manager of Hot Guitars, promoter of The Cimarons, and associated with Joe O'Donnell, so they all went on the same bill with Rory for this concert.

I found a stone-cutter who used offcuts of marble to make pieces like trophies for the bands we worked with. I wanted them

to remember Ireland's first Rock festival. The Cimarons thought they had received an Oscar, they were so delighted. We also gave one to RTÉ's Ken Stewart who was the MC. Later we presented one to the directors of the festival. It was a simple memento to show our gratitude for what they had done.

In 1978 *Hot Press* created the Hot Press Awards which I suggested should come from a readers' poll. The Kiss Me Quick award was going to Johnny Rotten (John Lydon) which is why he travelled on a flight with us from the UK. The German film crew was getting footage on the flight over and obligingly Aer Lingus had removed seats to accommodate the cameras. After a delay in finding Rotten in the bar in the airport, he arrived, and when people saw him they wanted to get off the plane. Despite being offered a seat with us, he sat with two nuns, one elderly, one young. He made them feel particularly uncomfortable when under his big coat he revealed he was dressed as a priest. There was nearly a mutiny on the plane. When we arrived in Cork we were keen to play down the fuss as an arrest would have played into

Rotten's hand and, even though he wasn't our responsibility at all, would have been bad publicity for the festival.

A press area around the stage had been created and I went to Woolworths in Cork and bought replica medals that I gave to everyone as backstage passes.

Despite the hospitality shown, a few of the guests seemed to be there just to get attention for themselves. A PR man was trying to generate publicity against Johnny Rotten by intending to throw a bucket of waste, generated by earlier bands caught short, over the equipment. So we took the bucket away, giving him fair warning, and highlighting the dangers with all the electrics around. Ignoring the warning, he was ejected and his cry was "They're throwing out all the punks, come on Johnny, they don't want punks here!" He got the attention he wanted from the media and ended up on the front pages. It was upsetting and annoying and, while they may not have meant any harm, took away from a very successful concert. Compare this with a decent young Edge who had bought his own ticket and was there to appreciate the music!

However, it all adds to the legend that the Macroom Festival has since become.

Jenny Haan

1978

" The Macroom Mountain Dew Festival was very memorable for me as it was the last gig Jenny Haan's Lion played. It was very bittersweet. John Lydon and Bob Geldof were there and of course Rory Gallagher. I was pretty devastated at that time as I was bulldozed by Status Quo management to go solo, and for us it was all heartbreaking to be ending our relationship. Pressure from the music industry, sigh ... I remember after we played, going to see Rory and there were talks of us recording together which sadly never came to fruition. The day itself was like a blur and I barely talked all day – I loved my band. I remember coming offstage and we were back in the band's caravan we were given for that day, and Bob Geldof poked his head round the door. I don't remember what he said!

I have very happy feelings when I think of Macroom. It's funny as both Rory Gallagher and myself are very shy people off stage. When we met we were terribly polite and shy. I'm now part of Heroes – United Artists Against Terrorism which was formed after the Paris attacks. "

Jenny Haan *Courtesy John L Taylor*

Mike Lowe

1977 & 1978

"Based in London, my company, Britannia Row, provided the sound systems for Rory Gallagher's concerts both years. I remember Macroom as I had always enjoyed my visits to Ireland. Though I have yet to meet my relatives, I grew up in Liverpool and am a quarter Irish through my grandmother Mollie Healy from Kerry. I am just about to start tracing my relatives.

I remember being aware that this was the first open-air Rock concert in Ireland. We had done quite a few in the US and UK so we brought with us reasonably new technology which hadn't yet been seen in Ireland. To get the flow of sound right we had to be creative in our thinking as we needed height. We organised towers to be built. These days you have sophisticated flying hoists and all sorts to get equipment into place. We had to use a block and tackle, all from the front. We used some acrow props to deal with some gaps in the pile of pallets already in place, and we put some under lintels and a few more bits to make it right for us. I had already worked with sound engineer Joe O'Herlihy who was there for both of Rory's concerts and we had Jonathan Glinos front of house on the mixing console. I think we got a pretty good sound, alright. As you said, people were delighted when they could hear the sound in villages 12 miles away. They wouldn't like that these days, you'd be shot! It's all about avoiding noise pollution. However, we did a Bob Dylan and a Paul Simon concert in Kilkenny, and we kept the noise so well channelled that some people were disappointed with the 'low' volume. With a good weather forecast, they had arranged barbecue parties to enjoy the music and they asked us to turn it up! The Irish love a party.

I remember that in the first of Rory's two gigs in Macroom, the numbers coming to the concert were so underestimated that the chippers ran out of potatoes. We sent our driver off in one of the trucks back to the UK where he loaded up with potatoes and brought them to us overnight. It was incredible that the town really didn't have a clue what to expect of this event – the numbers certainly exceeded expectations.

We are always trying to improve sound quality, that's what keeps me interested. Now I get the younger members of the company to do the hard work that I did back forty years ago at the time of the Mountain Dew Festival."

Roland Van Campenhout

1977

" I still have my trophy for playing at the First Irish Rock Festival, given to me by Dónal Gallagher. I don't have a mantelpiece any more, but I treasure it. My relationship with Rory Gallagher started with one show in France, maybe in Metz, and it went so well he invited me to do the rest of the French tour, including the Paris Olympia. After that he and Dónal and the band stayed for a while in our Ghent studio.

I remember the Mountain Dew Festival and have always loved Ireland. Rory Gallagher said there were similarities between Belgian and Irish country living, and he was right. I have always enjoyed going there and did a cookery television programme in Ballymaloe House for a Belgian network. I loved Kinsale too and wrote a song, Stars above Kinsale, about it.

I usually play solo gigs so it's easy to travel in the same car with the other acts. I play the harmonica and blues on guitar, using an echo chamber. I often ended up jamming with Rory on stage.

I always liked the folk influences of the US and UK and India, such as Ravi Shankar.

At the Mountain Dew Festival I remember some U2 members hanging around and Joe O'Herlihy who worked with us and now works with them. I thank Rory for taking me to the Montreux festival in Switzerland, the schooling he gave me, and the good times. I could cry right now. When I play I use his strength. His body is gone, but his soul is still here. No-one played like him. He was a category to himself.

Now I like to play in smaller venues. The big ones have become too sanitised. I spend my money on guitars and old records and that's the way I like it, but it means I don't get to Ireland as much as I want. I miss it. Someone said "I have never seen a hearse with money", so it's time to get back there. "

> *We were all young, and to be sharing the stage with Rory was amazing. He was a mountain.*
>
> **Joe O'Donnell, 1978**

Joe O'Herlihy

1977 & 1978

"Dónal (Gallagher) came in one day and said, "Macroom Mountain Dew Festival have been on and they want us to play there and they want to have the first Rock festival in Ireland." They were pioneers of their time. Dónal grasped the nettle and we ended up doing everything you could possibly do from a technical point of view in the entire production aspect of things. You were kind of told, "There's a field, the rest is yours. You figure it out from there!"

Áine O'Connor and Shay Healy Cork Examiner/Evening Echo

Tony Milner

1977

"I was just ten when I played at the festival. I was part of Farranree Boys' School Band from Scoil Íosagáin in Cork. Our teacher Billy Clifford was our school band conductor and we were invited to open the 1977 festival. We were the lead band – I don't remember if there were others – and we marched all the way up the town and through the Castle gates. I remember how imposing those gates were. I thought that this must have been how wonderful it was to be in a St Patrick's Day parade.

The band was about thirty strong and I was playing the tin whistle. We also had Melodicas (there's a blast from the past!) with two drums keeping beat as we played The Cork March and The Minstrel Boy. We wore white shirts, our school ties and cloth cadet-like caps. We were whisked away quickly and I never got to see Rory Gallagher who was probably performing on a different day anyway. I didn't really know who he was, but I like to think I was on the same bill as him. At least I can say we played at the same festival, in the same year!

On the way back I remember bonfires everywhere as it was Bonfire Night. It was incredible to see the flames along the journey as we were driven back to the school to be collected by our parents."

Map Castle grounds courtesy Dónal Gallagher

Ted McKenna

1978, Rory Gallagher Band

"I joined Rory's band a few weeks before the Macroom festival. It came as a result of a friend, fellow drummer and engineer, Colin Fairley, telling me that Rory was looking for a drummer and was holding auditions. The timing was right as I had just left another band. I remember going to see Rory during a Taste gig when he played sax. In those days I would go along to gigs and stand up in the balcony to watch the drummers and girls!

I played with him a few times back in 1967. We used to change our clothes in our van, as Rory did in his. I just remembered him as a nice chap. When I walked into the studio for the audition in 1978, he was the exact same Rory. I remember reading a review in the *Melody Maker* where it was suggested that Rory's casual dress style was a bit affected. It was nonsense. He always dressed that way, all through the years. That day of the audition I brought my own drum kit and hauled it up a few flights of stairs. I played for about an hour, some jams and grooves, and when I was leaving Rory and Dónal insisted on helping me downstairs with all my gear. That's how decent they were. I went up to Scotland to visit my parents and a few days later Dónal rang me and asked if we could rehearse soon. It was a completely different vibe to The Sensational Alex Harvey Band (SAHB). I had played with them for five years during which time we had recorded nine albums (I recorded three with Rory in three years). SAHB was theatrical and had its own rhythm. With Rory it was full-on for the two hours of a gig. We never knew what he was going to do. Like Gerry McAvoy, I became part of the chemistry of the performance. He played a song differently every time, so we had to adjust and if I may say so myself, that's what I have always been able to do.

Rehearsing before the Macroom gig was exhausting, but then we moved up a gear for the performance. The fans were crazy about Rory. He was a huge asset to Ireland. It went very well. I remember Rory falling into a chair after it! It's easy for your fitness to go if you haven't been playing, your heart quickens and later, when you get back into gigging, it slows down and you feel fit again. That time in Macroom I ended up with water blisters on my hand from playing lots of encores. I remember at times feeling so fit I could have fought Muhammed Ali. My Irish grandfather was a booth fighter, travelling from town to town and challenging the toughest man to fight him for money. A night off would consist of hanging around playing cards, having a laugh and drinking, as I often did with Rory. I remember the odd time having such a hangover that I could hear someone up in the sound booth scratching his face! But I never drank before or during a gig that I was being paid to do, I might during a jam session, but not otherwise.

I enjoyed Roland Van Campenhout coming on stage for one of our encores, and I think it was for 'I Got My Mojo Working' that I had a kind of out-of-body experience. It was like I was looking down on myself. I could see people jumping up and down to the beat of a snare drum. I was playing all the time, but when you have that chemistry, it's like an instinct and you keep going.

I grew up in a musical family. My great-grandfather came from Co Monaghan and I have loads of relatives, there are ninety heads of families there! When we stayed in Coolcower House, it was my first time in Ireland and it was just as I expected it to be. I remember walking around the gardens in the evening. It was warm and sunny and I could picture Maureen O'Hara and John Wayne in *The Quiet Man*. That was my image of Ireland and that was what I saw for the few evenings we rehearsed in the house.

'The Last of the Independents' is Rory to me. He could have been bigger if he had listened to his record company, but in the end I'm not convinced he would have been the better for it. He didn't need them, which was his strength.

Nowadays, music is devalued. Free music online is all very well, but it's not good for the industry. When I was playing five times a week when I was at school, I had more money to spend! As Rory used to say, "Performance is the meat and potatoes", and that's what we do more of now. And as my cousin Hugh says, "Fame is a game; music is an art". I play with Gerry McAvoy in Band of Friends and we are busy on the road gigging. I do other session recordings from time to time, as well as writing songs. There will be a Band of Friends album, and I'm writing a book about my life, which is difficult to do when you are on the road, but I try to take notes as I go. I got a little advice about various aspects of the process from Ian Rankin who was a great fan of Rory's. I never get tired of playing the same tunes as they're so good. My electronic drum kit is in the living room and I still practice. **"**

Johnny Lappin
1978

" I was tour manager for Joe O'Donnell in 1978 and managed Stepaside who performed that year too. In 1975 I had started in music publishing and recorded other acts of the festival – The Atrix and The Rhythm Kings. I also run Clannad Music, though I wasn't on the road with them when they played at the festival.

I remember the festival so well as Joe O'Donnell was being managed by Dónal Gallagher and I had flown down to Cork to meet him before getting my job on the tour. That flight made me feel very sophisticated so I thought I was where it was at. At the time of the festival itself, I was driving a Ford Capri and arrived there in it. I had sent the band's equipment ahead of me on the train and arranged for it to be picked up and brought to Macroom. It was all going to plan until I arrived and checked up on it. Only half of it was in place. I was not happy. Time was moving on and this needed to be sorted. I eventually tracked down the farmer who had used his tractor and trailer to transport it. I found him in his farmhouse calmly having his lunch. "I'll deliver it after I have finished my lunch," he said. "There's no effin' lunch in Rock 'n Roll!," I railed at the farmer who was horrified at my outburst. It was my first gig as a tour manager and I was keen to impress. I had kudos just being involved with Dónal Gallagher and I didn't need setbacks like this. Of course it all turned out alright and the gig went very well. It was an important festival – a big thing – an open-air festival that was completely new to Ireland. I have a high regard for it. It was a seminal part of Irish history and should be remembered for that. "

Joe O'Donnell

1978

" I attended the festival the year before I played in it. In 1977 I was just backstage, ligging. I brought my *Gaodhal's Vision* records with me and sold out completely at a stall I set up. They played it over the sound system all the time. I was kind of being head-hunted by another record label which was very flattering, but I stuck with Polydor and it was John Woods of that record company who set up the festival gig. I was just starting becoming better known. In 1978 I was living in Bray and the rest of the Vision band came from London. We rehearsed together in Macroom. It was a real rush as we hadn't done many gigs together. I was okay as I hadn't far to travel and I wasn't a tourist in Macroom like many other people, so I was very focused on the music. The gig was like a giant poitín bottle, full of energy ready to be released. In fact, we were on such a high that we wondered if our pints had been spiked with Mountain Dew! It was just great. A huge adventure. It was all about the stage and the pub afterwards where everyone wanted to exchange telephone numbers. People knew my music by then as the album had done well.

We were all young, and to be sharing the stage with Rory was amazing. He was a mountain. Great! I had got up on stage to play with him from time to time and he played on my album *Gaodhal's Vision*. He and his brother Dónal were very good to me and to many musicians. I am classically trained so I do my scales – major, minor and Indian – at least five days a week, both on the violin and the mandolin. I haven't drunk alcohol for 12 years and feel the better for it. We drank quite a lot at that festival! These days I perform, record and compose in Coventry. "

Nick Payne

Q-Tips 1981

"It's always nice to play festivals, and Q-Tips was a fantastic band to be in at them, especially in Ireland. I remember speaking to the Gardaí who were worried about the kind of crowd that might come to see The Undertones. They thought they might bring to their nice town a rough crowd of supporters from the North where they came from. Given the times that were in it, there could have been trouble. In fact there wasn't. We generally went down well as we were a good live act, not just Paul Young, but all of us. I think people liked the strong brass line-up, at least that's what they told us!

In the late sixties I used to share the stage with Rory Gallagher when he was in Taste. We often supported them in pubs and clubs. I was part of Union Blues. Taste produced fantastic music. They knocked me out. Rory had an incredible feel for music.

I was glad to be in Macroom and enjoyed my stay. My second cousin Patsy Dyke was married to the late Cathal O'Shannon so after the gig I managed to get a bus from Macroom to Limerick to meet them and my great aunt before leaving on the ferry.

I've been to the Cork Jazz Festival lots of times since then and have played in Cork Opera House as part of a jazz quartet. I played with Georgie Fame, the Boomtown Rats, Bill Wyman's Rhythm Kings and with Lonnie Donegan who is one of the reasons I started to play music. He proved that you don't have to be a trained musician to be able to play.

During some of those gigs I got to eat Kinsale oysters. Ireland has plenty to offer, and Macroom is one of my nicer experiences there."

Nick Payne and Steve Farr, Q-Tips
Cork Examiner/Evening Echo

Paul Charles

1978

" I earned a Green Jacket before Rory McIroy was even born.

I'm a partner in the Asgard Agency which represents a lot of artists worldwide. I first heard about the Macroom Mountain Dew Festival when Rory Gallagher played at it in 1978. Rory and his brother Dónal were ahead of the pack. They had so many firsts on their CV. One of the really big ones, because of what has happened with festivals and outdoor events in Ireland since, was being the first act, national or international, to headline an Irish music festival.

We'd a show already planned for Van on the same weekend as Macroom at the Kings Hall Showgrounds in Belfast – showing just how quickly Rory, Donal and the Mountain Dew's committee's idea for this outdoor malarkey was catching on. A deal was concluded for Van to appear at Macroom on 29th June 1980. The ticket price was £8.

We arrived at the Macroom site and the driver didn't know where to go, so he drove us in through the audience's entrance of the Castle, as close as possible to the stage. Van just hopped out of the car and walked unnoticed through the crowd. On the way into the back stage area he hit himself in the mouth while ducking underneath one of the scaffolding bars supporting the security fence. He lost a crown of one of his front teeth and we left several of his crew members searching for it in the grass.

In 1981 the Macroom committee's idea for that year's Mountain Dew Festival was that I would programme the entire bill for them. So I booked Elvis Costello & The Attractions, The Undertones, Paul Brady & His Band, The Rhythm Kings, Sniff 'n' the Tears, Moondogs, Q-Tips and Scullion to appear on the Saturday and Sunday.

I remember Elvis & The Attractions playing an amazing, barnstorming set and Elvis' voice being totally shot by the end of it. There were few better live bands than The Undertones on the circuit in those days, and boy did they live up to their reputation. For some reason The Pretenders didn't show up, so we juggled around the programme and The Undertones were promoted to top of the bill on the second day. Dave Fanning was the DJ and kept everyone happy between acts, doing what he does so well.

The Mountain Dew Festival committee wore matching green jackets at their official meetings and they kindly presented me with one that year. I remember feeling just like Jack Nicklaus at Augusta, getting my green jacket, seven years before Rory McIroy was born. **"**

Oliver Kane
1978, West Cork Band

" I play in lots of bands and may have played in more than one during the Mountain Dew Festival over the years. I replaced Rory Gallagher in the Fontana showband, but didn't manage to get to his gig in Macroom. I had often played in Martin Fitz-Gerald's pub, The Hooded Cloak, and during the festival after playing in The Dome which was close to it, we played upstairs in the Oak Room. We developed a following and people would come and go during the night.

I was sorry I didn't get to see Elvis Costello as I had met his mother, Rose McManus. When I was 16, I went to London to escape home and make my own way, and worked in The Wellington pub, opposite Waterloo Bridge and next to the Lyceum ballroom. The members of the resident band would come next door to us to relax after work, and I was invited one evening to hear the singer. It was Elvis's mother and what a beautiful voice she had.

I was always interested in playing the guitar so I bought a Fender Stratocaster and equipment to go with it with my first few weeks' wages and taught myself to play it. I eventually came home with it and joined the Fontana first, then a number of other bands.

For the Mountain Dew Festival I was part of the West Cork Band which consisted of Gerry Lane of Driveshaft, Mick O'Donovan, Patrick O'Donovan, Paddy Noonan and The Lawlor Brothers. For me the Oak Room in The Hooded Cloak was a centrepoint of futuristic music, a place where musicians could express themselves. You'd let a percussionist flake it out for 10 minutes. It was like looking at a child playing. The Mountain Dew Festival brought a lot of musicians together. "

Marco Petrassi
1977 & 1978

" I remember playing in the Square in Macroom – I do that kind of thing a lot – it brings people in, the activity, the music coming from all angles. I didn't have time to go to concerts, and I really didn't want to, it was like working. I love playing the trumpet and am often asked to play in different bands. It's a great career to have and at the Macroom festival I played in a few which I really liked as every night felt different. I'm glad you are writing this book – people should be reminded of all that went on. "

Maddy Prior
1980

" I had my own band for the festival, despite having performed with Steeleye Span at various times at that period. I was pregnant then and think I remember meeting the gang, such as Christy Moore and the Fureys whom I had met in Australia. I remember walking late at night on the lawn out front of the hotel (Coolcower). I don't remember much about the gig itself, but it's always good to play in Ireland. We always have good fun. These days I do Steeleye gigs often in the US, and also work as part of a trio with Giles Lewin and Hannah James and with the Carnival Band. "

Paul Roberts
1981, Sniff 'n' The Tears

" I remember the festival well. We were on in the afternoon just after The Blues Band. There was a rowdy element in front of the stage chucking bottles and generally misbehaving. Our guitarist Les Davidson dealt with this by duck walking, doing guitar hero stuff and generally ramping up the energy, which seemed to work and he got the crowd with us. Elvis Costello, on later, engaged in a stand-off with them, refusing to play until they stopped, which I seem to remember went on for quite a while with slow hand claps and everything. Meanwhile, people were being stretchered out of the area in front of the stage. He did play in the end and his performance was written up by Alan Jones in the *Melody Maker* as 'a triumph', whereas we were 'over the top, with a guitarist who looked like an inmate from Rampton psychiatric hospital'. I wondered if he was there at all, but later the same day in the bar of the hotel, I spotted Alan Jones in a huddle with Jake Riviera (Elvis's manager). Perhaps one lesson is to never play when fans come to hear someone else. There is a tribalism in music and sometimes the matches aren't quite right.

I met Paul Brady at the festival and went to see him recently in the Half Moon in Putney. My daughter plays accordion in a band and it seems like a good time for music, with people getting out and trying things. Our band is recording at the moment, with our bassist in LA and drummer in London working remotely, adding their tracks. It's all possible, unlike in the Mountain Dew days, when we had to be together to record. I'm not sure which is best. "

Greg Boland
Supply, Demand and Curve 1978;
Scullion 1981

" What stands out for me about the 1978 gig was meeting Rory Gallagher in Inchigeela. We were staying in the hotel there and we had long finished our gig and were hanging around in the foyer. Rory arrived after his gig and was not at all interested in the fuss and hangers-on, but was obsessed with guitars which is why he made a beeline for me.

I had met him six or nine months beforehand and discussed a problem I had with my guitar. He remembered and came over to check the outcome. His was a great concert, as usual. He was a huge influence on me and many others. I remember Q-Tips in 1981 as we played on the same bill as them several times. I've probably done four or five thousand gigs at this stage, so it's not easy to remember all of them. I do remember being in the Metropole Hotel in Cork earlier in 1981. I'm a big Spurs fan and they won that night, and we played afterwards straight after it. That was a good night! "

Cork Examiner/Evening Echo

Keith Donald

1982, Moving Hearts

" I have all my own diaries from way back, with notes about what women I was with, about my daughter, where we played. We were recording our second album with Christy Moore at Ridge Farm in the UK at the time of the Mountain Dew Festival. My diary reads: "25 June left Ridge Farm 7.30am. Travelled ex Fishguard to Cork. Arrived Metropole Hotel 10pm. Saturday 26th played Macroom, back to Metropole Hotel, 27th to Mullingar." That doesn't tell you a lot about the festival, more about the busy schedule we had. What I remember about Macroom is the thrill of it. I was conscious of an atmosphere of excitement – you don't always get that at festivals.

I am off the booze for 25 years now. In those days I never drank beforehand but could consume a bottle of vodka on stage and it would have no effect. Apparently, I never missed a note! The saxophone is a difficult instrument to play with the uilleann pipes, as they can only be played in the keys of A and E. I have to play three or four sharps, which is tricky.

For Macroom, Davy Spillane as usual was on the pipes, Donal Lunny on guitar, Christy Moore singing, Declan Sinnott on mandolin, Eoghan O'Neill on bass, Matt Kelleghan on drums. Coming off drink was tough, as it is for everyone suffering from an addiction. Since I have been off it, with a lot of help from my great daughter and the AA and others, I am enjoying gigging and am still doing so with Moving Hearts. I am also chairman of the Irish Music Rights Organisation (IMRO). I do a one-man show 'NewBliss' which is a musical memoir in which I talk about the effect alcohol had on my career and my redemption. It gets easier as the years go on. I celebrated my 71st birthday (in 2016) where I live, in the Dublin mountains. "

John Sheehan

The Cimarons

1978. Franklyn Dunn, Carl Levy, Locksley Gichie and Maurice Ellis in group interview

"We came to Britain from Jamaica in 1967. We were the first reggae band to play in Ireland and had always gone down well on the Northern Ireland college circuit. No pop groups would go to Northern Ireland during The Troubles. We were nervous, but not afraid. We just loved to play. On one trip we were about to start and we could see divisions in the crowd and were told they were the Protestants at one side of the hall and Catholics at the other. Winston (Reid) our vocalist, announced that we wouldn't perform unless the two sides came together. They did and we had a high energy night, as usual.

For our gig in the Mountain Dew Festival we had to fly back to Scotland on the same day, which was impossible with regular flights, so an eight-seater plane was chartered for us. It was a very rocky flight so we had to smoke our weed to calm us down. The space was so confined that we probably smelled of it a lot when we arrived. We took a chance bringing in our own stash and had no trouble at Customs, but we just missed going to jail in Macroom. We were stopped by a plain clothes officer who saw us smoking when we were amongst the crowd. He asked us where we had got our spliffs. We didn't have a clue as a fan had proudly given us his homemade ones. The fan said: "There you are, I've grown it myself. I call it Kerrygold!" That was real Irish hospitality! We Jamaicans are like the Irish. We make light of problems and enjoy ourselves. At these kinds of gigs we feel high anyway – there's no need for magic mushrooms!

Reggae is part of life in Jamaica. It started as Calypso, then Ska and Boogie. Reggae was an accident that happened and migrated. We always liked to jump around. Usually thirty minutes into the set we took off our hats and threw them in the air. Our hair would fall down and fly around our heads. People always went a bit wild, as they did in Macroom. We are getting old now and do less jumping around and our hair under our hats is grey! Winston, our lead singer, is the fittest as he performs all the time.

We had good fun in Macroom for the short time we were there. There was good energy. You can listen to all the albums you like, but there is nothing to beat a live band.

A final memory of our visit to Macroom is a trophy we got from Rory Gallagher. We played on the same bill as him at the festival. It was made of marble and it was like winning the Oscars. We still have it and it's a reminder of the good time we had in Macroom."

Locksley Gichie, Carl Levy, Winston Reid (Reedy) *John Sheehan*

Peadar O'Riada

1978–1980

Comhaltas Ceoltóirí Éireann

" The best thing about the festival for me was that it put me in contact with Fitzie. We have become good friends and he is as courageous and as mad as the rest of us.

Rory Gallagher's first cousins sang in our choir for the mass at the 1978 festival. Afterwards we went to Fitzie's for more fun. I had the feeling that while the festival was about Rock, it was culturally broader than that. In 1980 as Comhaltas Ceoltóirí Éireann, we did a recital on a platform in the Square on the first Saturday night of the festival. I had long hair in those days and often went to Sir Henry's in Cork. Lots of people would come and go. There was excitement with poverty. The bank strikes saved the nation. People passed cheques, put money into circulation – the quantitative easing of the 70s. We didn't know we were in a recession then. It always happened in Dublin anyway, not down here. We didn't have much money in the first place. We lived in each other's pockets in those days. If someone had enough money for a few drinks they would share it. We were more interested in drink and the craic, not drugs. We saw the Hippies come and go in Macroom and further west

in Cúil Aodha. The weather soon saw them off to Portugal. The weather always seemed to be dreary and damp. Normal. They were interesting times. The Troubles in the North meant that those of us who spoke Irish and were interested in Irish culture were seen as subversive. Up here in the mountains we are probably more Republican than elsewhere, and the Gardaí were aware of that and watched us with suspicion. I was acutely aware of surveillance. We had some aggressive approaches and were treated as second class citizens. That was the mood of the time.

The big stuff of the festival went on in the Castle grounds. We called it The Freak in the Park – joyous!

In those days we men from my area still wore our boleros and the women long skirts. We had no money for new cars and often filled the holes in our bangers with biscuit tins and used a pair of tights for a fan belt. The chipper was our idea of a restaurant and that's what was available at the festival. The pizza hadn't even arrived!

What I liked about the Mountain Dew Festival was its wide canvas. There was still common ground between the various musical traditions that celebrated our flourishing culture. You can see it in the huge talent all over the country and abroad. You would wander along the streets, planning to hear a concert, but getting distracted by people moving around, you would turn around after talking to someone and the time would be gone. I met a Russian man with a violin over his shoulder. He had broken English, but fluent Irish. There are 5,000 third level institutes in North America teaching Irish now.

I believe that to keep them fresh, festivals shouldn't be run every year. Féile na Laoch is run on a seven-year cycle. The next one will be in 2018. **"**

Lá de's na ceire fichid a bhí ann le ceol agus ól, aoibhneas agus iontas, is dea-mhéinn agus dea-thoil ag gach n'aon ag gabháil tímpeal i lár MhághCromtha.

Peadar O'Riada

Cork Examiner/Evening Echo

Mike Murphy

1977, 1978 & 1980 RTÉ

" I remember the Mountain Dew Festival very well. I was buried at it! Why I agreed to it, I don't know. I think I was experimenting at the time. I had gone into a lion's den and jumped out of a plane. It was part of the curriculum of my life. At the time I wasn't as famous as Frank Hall. He opened the festival in 1977 and we had great banter.

Tim Hayes from Cobh had been buried alive for 100 hours in 1967 and was in the Guinness Book of Records. He came along to support me and I asked him for advice. "Don't let your legs get itchy. You won't be able to reach them," was his reply. He was right: there was no room for manoeuvre, I really couldn't scratch. I was lowered into the ground with great ceremony, the heavy lid had been closed already. I don't know why I didn't mind, but I didn't. I had full confidence I would be looked after. I was lowered a long way down. I know because it took 20 minutes to haul me up. There was a hole in the coffin and a tube reached up out of the grave so people could talk to me. They kept me company with all sorts of questions and remarks. They paid for the privilege.

The time passed quickly as I thought I was there for about 45 minutes, but people tell me I was there for three hours. At one point a 'smart Alec' blocked the pipe which cut out the little bit of light coming in. It also blocked off my air supply which was not funny at all. In those days I didn't get nervous. I wouldn't do it now. I wouldn't let my son do it if he suggested it, but it was an unusual way to spend an hour or two. I was the only sucker to fall for the idea, but I admired the imagination of the committee members who thought it up and the other schemes which publicised the festival.

When I was finally brought up over-ground, I went around the town with Anthony Murphy into various pubs and the place was buzzing. There was a great festive atmosphere. I went back to the festival the following year to officiate at the opening and again in 1980. They were enjoyable occasions. "

Paddy McCarthy

1977-1982, Sunset

" I was a promoter as well as a drummer and had brought quite a few bands to Cork. I often worked with Quarry Management, a company working with Status Quo and Rory Gallagher. I knew Rory well already and was involved in contacting Dónal Gallagher about him coming to the first Macroom Mountain Dew Festival. At the same time Martin Fitz-Gerald was talking to Rory's mother, so between us, it all worked out well. My band Sunset got on the bill with Rory as a result. At that time with me were the late Eric Kitteringham on bass – he had played in Taste with Rory, and before that in The Axills. We all knew each other on the Cork scene. Tony Sullivan was on lead guitar and Donie Searls sang.

We opened the first Rory concert which was fantastic for us with all their great equipment. We couldn't believe the crowds – 17,000 at least! We played seven songs, including three original numbers and went down well. When Rory got onto the stage, he pulled me up and presented me with a trophy and told the crowd that we were the first band of the first open-air Rock concert in Ireland. That was a huge moment. Out of this world! That first day, we were so badly off that we hitched home. Not so glamorous after such a great gig. We didn't care.

We did lots of gigs over the years of the festival. I was the person who lifted Ronnie Drew up onto the stage – he had a problem with one of his legs at the time. The Dubliners did an unbelievable gig. We were always willing to stand in if someone didn't turn up, so one way or another we were often on in The Dome. There was always good gear there. We did another open-air gig in Coolcower. I didn't like that location as much – the festival should have stayed in the Castle grounds. I am based in NYC now where I publish the online *Irish Examiner* newspaper. I don't play music, but look back on the festival years as a great time. "

Pipe bands can only be judged on grass to ensure consistent acoustics.

Con Houlihan

Claire Lutter and Jane Eve, Love Machine

1978

"We arrived for our rehearsal in the afternoon, which included Teresa, Libby, Lorraine, Nick our road manager/sound technician and Ricky, Lorraine's boyfriend. Jane was at the hotel as she wasn't well. The stage was not suitable for us, it was very small and made of rough timber and there was a six-foot drop from the stage to the tented dressing room area.

Nick said it was not what we had agreed and we could not perform. However, it seemed that a great deal of drink had already been consumed and perhaps it was a disappointment that we weren't a band, so the atmosphere became quite hostile and Nick was told, "if the girls don't perform tonight, you won't get out of here alive". We did a quick rehearsal of a slightly shortened show and went back to the hotel to collect Jane, returning to perform at The Dome.

We were all worried throughout the performance as there seemed to be a lot of pushing and shoving from the mainly male, very inebriated audience, but it was certainly a memorable night and perhaps in hindsight at times farcical. To get off the stage to our dressing area, for our very quick changes, we needed Ricky to haul us up and down a ladder, on a couple of occasions even throwing ourselves into his arms! We would normally perform a pas de deux in bare feet but decided, because of the state of the stage, to wear our high shoes. Jane forgot about that and stayed in bare feet, so we both performed the lyrical dance with a big height discrepancy, which was quite comical.

It had been decided that we would leave as quickly as possible after the show, so as soon as we finished Nick backed the van to the entrance to our changing tent, we came off stage without changing, threw all the costumes into the back of the van and escaped."

"Macroom", said the old man in the town Square, "will never be the same again. Even the Redemptorists could not boast of anything like it during the General Mission in my boyhood days".

Larry Lyons, The Cork Examiner, 1977

Brendan Grace

1978

" Okay, if my memory serves me correctly I was doing my stint on the Sunday. I had just had a Number One in the charts with the Shay Healy-penned Cushy Butterfield and a hugely successful spot on The Late Late Show where I introduced Bottler for the first time. But the thought of performing live to thousands of would-be hippies in Macroom was terrifying. So taking the stage was like diving into Bantry Bay naked on Christmas Day!

My comedian hat was used a lot less than my ballad hat, as I belted out plenty of 'Wild Rovers' and 'Black Velvet Bands'. Incidentally, my assistant roadie then was a funny little wiry young fella be the name of Brendan O'Carroll who much later in life would have a sex change operation – in fact a very successful one indeed – to become Mrs Brown. We drank the night away in a well-known hostelry called The Hooded Cloak. We slept the night in our VW van and I woke up to the wafting aroma of rashers and sausages. It was a surreal atmosphere, like I've never experienced before or since. "

Joe O'Callaghan

1978, Hot Guitars

" We played in the Castle grounds a good bit before Rory Gallagher. We would like to have been on just before him, but The Cimarons had that slot and they were excellent. The dreadlocks and the colours of the rainbow of their hats added to the fun. Also after us was Stepaside. I gave my harmonica to one of them – Brendan Bonass.

I had been living in Dublin and we came to Cork for the festival. We had brought out a single ('Nasty People/Route 66') and had some following. People arrived for our gig, but nothing like it was for Rory Gallagher, of course. It was a big stage, a big field, very open, and you were quite far away from those listening. We were just a four piece then with Bill O'Brien, Brian Calnan, Johnny Rice and myself. You just do the best you can in those situations. I had just come back from London and had gone to the festivals in the Isle of Wight – Jethro Tull etc – and the atmosphere seemed better there than at Macroom, but we enjoyed seeing Bob Geldof there and Johnny Rotten, a country squire now, being very rude. We were there when the German film crew, making a film about Rory, came along. That was interesting to watch. "

Paul Brady
1979, 1980 & 1981

" I played at Macroom Mountain Dew Festival three times: in 1979 solo and then in '80 and '81 with my band. The first one in '79 was a folk gig with The Fureys, Dubliners, Paddy Reilly and Jim McCann. I really enjoyed that day and, according to a press review, made a big impression on the crowd.

In 1980 I had started writing the songs that became the album *Hard Station* and I had put an electric band together. I mostly remember the 1980 gig with Van Morrison, Mike Oldfield, The Chieftains and Lindisfarne. The talking point of the day was Van coming to the field beside the backstage area and demanding a limo to take him the 50 yards to the stage! Also there was a major incursion to the site during my set when a fence at the top of the hill collapsed and dozens of people ran in for free. It somewhat took away from my gig with most people turning round to get a look!

The 1981 gig doesn't really stand out in my memory though I remember the line-up: myself and band, Elvis Costello, The Undertones, The Blues Band (I sang a song with them), Scullion, Q-Tips, The Rhythm Kings and Sniff 'n' the Tears. Great times and a great festival! "

Eddie O'Hare Cork Examiner/Evening Echo

Barney McKenna, John Sheahan, Ronnie Drew, Luke Kelly *Cork Examiner/Evening Echo*

John Sheahan
1979 & 1982, The Dubliners

" I remember a sunny afternoon of the Mountain Dew Festival, and have a vivid memory of Jim McCann bringing a cool bag filled with bottles of white wine into the stage area. We were always a happy band and people seemed to respond to that and come with us. We had a divil-may-care attitude, take it or leave it, and they usually took us! We might get a slow handclap in Germany if we were late going on stage and we would wait until they finished the clapping, then we would amble on and convert them. At festivals like Macroom our attitude was generally relaxed and we would stay on, often playing at another venue in a town. It was a totally different attitude to many places which were less relaxed in themselves anyway. Macroom had plenty of places to play afterwards.

I'm kept busy these days, despite an attempt to retire! It keeps you young, the mind active. I write poetry and was recently commissioned to write a poem which I have set to fiddle and whistle music with the working title of 'Liffey Song'. I remember places and structures. I still have my pocket diaries from each year which show we played at the Macroom Mountain Dew Festival. "

Mick Foster

1979, Foster & Allen

"The Mountain Dew was the first of our big festivals. We had only started in 1975 and went pro in 1977. Playing on the same stage as Ronnie Drew and all them boys was a big experience for us. The weather was great and we were playing with household names like the late Jim McCann, the Furey Brothers and Davey Arthur. We met them all, though somehow we missed Paul Brady as I think we had another gig afterwards.

It was our first folk festival. The crowd was huge. I had met Ronnie Drew before. He was himself that day. No-one else was like him. If you heard him on the radio you knew exactly who you were listening to. You didn't have to wonder. We didn't go to the pub afterwards as neither of us were and still are not big drinkers. It was just the two of us on stage – Tony Allen on keyboards and me on the accordion. We didn't add to the duo until December 1982. There's huge interest in the accordion these days.

Forty years later we're still playing and often play in Cork in the Opera House and the Everyman. I'm still in touch with Donal Ring. There is an accordion playing fraternity and we keep in touch. I see kids of eight and nine playing and I can't believe how good they are.

Farming talk keeps you on the straight and narrow. I'm horse mad anyway! Breeding a winning horse and having a hit record are both rarities. If you knew what did it, you would have big successes. But when it happens you have to be brainy enough to take advantage of it and that's what makes success. I never jarred, I was never late and that has stood to me. As for the Mountain Dew, it was a great day for Foster & Allen."

Ted Moynihan

1979, Shampain

"We played in The Dome on 23rd June 1979 and the gig was recorded by Joe O'Herlihy. It was a great gig, we were happy with it musically. It was not completely full to the rafters, but we were well supported by the crowd and were delighted with it. I was with Gerry 'the Yank' McConnell, Tony Burke, Art Lorigan and Alex McCarthy. After that I headed off to Europe to gig there with another few bands, and now back in Cork I join my friends in bands when they ask me."

Lindisfarne, left to right; Rod Clements, Simon Cowe (front), Alan Hull, Ray Laidlaw, Ray Jackson *Southern Star*

Ray Laidlaw

1980, 1982, Lindisfarne

"In 1980, we were doing three or four shows in the UK and Ireland with Van Morrison, Mike Oldfield and The Chieftains and, compared to all of them, we were an unknown quantity at that time. However, we had gone down particularly well in Belfast when we opened for Mike Oldfield. This caused a bit of trouble with the management who didn't want the upstaging to happen again. The result was that we had to go on after Van Morrison in Macroom which was very unusual to follow such a big act. Of course, most of the fans were there for him and the crowd diminished down to a quarter for us. We didn't mind – we knew he was a hard act to follow.

We always got on well with The Chieftains. In fact, we always got on well with all of the performers. The various managers were the problem and caused the tension. We just got on with it and did as we were told. We were pleased with how it went though, as people knew our hits such as 'Meet Me at the Corner', 'Lady Eleanor', 'Run for Home', 'Fog on the Tyne'.

We were well looked after. It appeared to us that the general running was done by people inexperienced in running gigs, but that didn't take away from it. Everyone was inexperienced in those days. There was a funny incident which really cracked us up. One of our crew noticed a little old man, who looked like a farmer, hanging about the one caravan serving as a band room backstage, which Van Morrison had commandeered. We learned that Van had insisted on a decoy car so he could get away easily from all the fans. This man, who bore absolutely no resemblance to Van, had been picked from the phone book as they had the same surname. That was what we were told, anyway. Perhaps it was someone having a laugh on us. As it happened a decoy was hardly necessary. Van had fans, but not ones that would mob him to that extent.

These days I present a stage show, *The Lindisfarne Story*, with Billy Mitchell, which has music, film clips and stills. Another member of the original band has been joined by others to play as Lindisfarne and I play with them too from time to time.

I play occasionally at charity events with people such as Mark Knopfler and AC/DC's Brian Johnson and I do productions for a children's cancer foundation. I work with director and producer Geoff Wonfor. We did one on the Dingle Film Festival and passed through Macroom recently on our way back from it. A touch of nostalgia as we drove. Happy memories."

Claire Hamill

1981, Wishbone Ash

"I do recall the festival. What a great line-up! It doesn't surprise me that there were few women on the bill. The establishment of women writers and performers took much longer to embed itself. I was with my new husband and we went on a sightseeing tour around the ring of Kerry.

My grandma's name was Mary Catherine Brennan and she was born in Tralee, the eldest of 12 children. Seven were born in Valentia and five in Portclarence, England, the same village I was born in. In fact, I was born in my grandma's back bedroom. She was called Molly but we all called her Mother.

She was extremely musical, I get my music from her but really, her baby sister, my Auntie Patty had the best voice in the family. We would wait at every family party for Patty to sing but she was very coquettish, sometimes she would sing and sometimes she wouldn't, but it never held up the party!

The most popular Wishbone Ash song was probably 'Blowing Free'. I didn't sing on that one, but Laurie Wisefield and I wrote one of their best songs ever called 'Living Proof'. The crowds go mad for that one! It has kept my name alive in the history of the band, which is nice.

The festival was lovely, well organised and extremely friendly and I wouldn't have expected anything else.

In those days I used to wear butter on my legs to make them shine on stage. I can hear my granny saying, "yes, best Irish butter!"

We were blown away by the wild fuschia hedgerows. It inspired my song called 'Valentia', which is on my last album."

Eddie O'Hare, Cork Examiner/Evening Echo

Jim O'Neill

1981, RTÉ

"I ran part of my RTÉ 2 radio show on the stage at the 1981 festival and remember saying that 9,000 people attended that day in Coolcower. As a result of The Mountain Dew Festival I became friends with Noel Redding and his partner Carol Appleby (both of them no longer with us). I played music then myself and joined in sessions in Shanleys and De Barras in Clonakilty from time to time. At that Sunday concert I remember Paul Brady, Paul Young and Q-Tips and Scullion. It was a terrific line-up."

Noel Redding, Carol Appleby, Jim O'Neill *Cork Examiner/Evening Echo*

Tom McGuinness

1981, Blues Band

"I have family in West Cork so I get over often to visit my 22 aunts and uncles who, with the exception of one nun, had about twelve children each. I have lots of cousins, the Hayes (O'Heas) and visit as many as possible when I get to Clonakilty and Glandore. My grandfather was a seanchaí whose stories are included in a UCD publication.

I have fantastic memories of Macroom. We were to play there on Saturday and in Switzerland the next day. Two small executive jets were hired for us – we were hot at the time – though this was still unusual for us, and we flew into Cork. My son Aaron, who was eight at the time, took up the only available spare seat and came with us. We landed in Cork Airport and decided we had better declare our music gear – guitars etc – as we didn't want any delay when we were leaving the next day in a rush. We unloaded our trollies, but there was no-one in the Customs' hall so we were told to go over to a little hut where we found the customs' officer drinking tea. We asked him to check our gear in. He looked around and said, "Do you have any dangerous drugs?" I replied that we didn't, but that Elvis Costello would be coming in later and he would probably have some!

My 81-year old aunt, Ellen Lyons, was at the concert. We were on in the early evening which was ideal for her at her age, and it turned out to be good for us, too, as the gig went well and we got a lot of media coverage. The journalists could write about us and still meet their print deadline. We got a double page spread in one newspaper which included a picture of my aunt. When she was asked if she liked my band, with that wonderful fearless directness that is the luxury of older people, she replied: "I wouldn't cross the road to hear them, but that's my nephew playing the guitar." For me that festival was very much a family occasion. I didn't hang around as I wanted Aaron to see as much family as possible, including my cousins Michael and Kitty Lyons. I remember Paul Brady, though, as he sang a chorus of one of our songs, probably 'Maggie's Farm', which was quite an anthem for us then and a big singalong number for the audience.

We got back to stay near Cork Airport and the next morning jetted off to Switzerland (in strong crosswinds), seeing snow on the Alps, played the gig and got back to London for Sunday night. My son went to school the next day where they had one of those Show 'n' Tell sessions. When he told the class what he had done for the weekend, the teacher

accused him of telling lies! These days I still play with The Blues Band and also with my former one, The Manfreds, a spin-off of Manfred Mann which I played in before The Blues Band . We played in Vicar Street in Dublin in March 2016.

Noel Redding was an old friend who lived just outside Clonakilty. My cousin Joe Lyons was his postman. When I told Joe that I was going to visit Noel, he said "Be careful, I do believe there might be drugs out there!"

I'm fascinated with the ancient history of West Cork and I get back as often as I can to catch up on the hundreds of relatives. The Mountain Dew Festival line-up was lead singer Paul Jones, singer/bass guitarist Gary Fletcher, the other short-sleeved singer guitarist was Dave Kelly, and the drummer was Hughie Flint. Amazingly, after 37 years, it's still almost the same line-up. Only Hughie left to be replaced by Rob Townsend in 1982.

Blues Band l-r: Dave Kelly, Gary Fletcher, Paul Jones, Tom McGuinness *John Sheehan*

Ferdia McAnna

1981 & 1982, Rocky de Valera and The Rhythm Kings, from an article written by Rocky de Valera for In Dublin Magazine, 27 May 1982

" We drove down to Macroom last year, crammed into a tiny van, band members, roadies and girlfriends squeezed between amplifiers and guitar cases, moaning and cursing at every bump in the road. Ritchie, Southside Geno and the Individual played poker all the time keeping up a running commentary of verbal abuse to quieten those in the cheap seats. Ritchie kept losing his shirt. "God Almighty, I've a hand like a foot,", he'd say as he looked at his cards. It was the kind of game nobody won, because the money kept ending up on the floor, never to be seen again.

The first thing I remember about the Macroom festival site was its size. It seemed tiny – just a hollow field with a covered stage in one corner. People were still trickling in, nosing the ground looking for mud-free patches to call home. Others, usually wearing Motorhead T-shirts, flopped down anywhere, getting themselves tuned up for the expected barrage of mud, blood, beer and Rock 'n' Roll.

We were the first band on that day, and we took to the stage to a half-full field and strange, vicious looking rainclouds bobbing

Irish Examiner/Evening Echo

overhead like vampires waiting for the midnight bell. We played for thirty minutes and went down well. I remember being able to spot familiar faces in the audience, dancing, catcalling and, in one case, giving me the finger. It was like playing in your back garden.

The backstage beer tent was a hotel hidden in the woods where musicians, roadies, managers, promoters, liggers and other assorted dorks hung out and drank themselves catatonic. Some people just sat at the bar the whole time, listening to reports of the festival, quizzing others who'd seen the bands and eventually going home convinced they'd seen a tremendous series of concerts. It was reasonably easy to sort out who was who backstage: anyone sweating or dishevelled was a musician just finished onstage – dudes who looked worried were managers, people in T-shirts and knuckledusters were bouncers, all roadies walked at seventy mph, and anyone with a can of beer in their hand was a personal friend of the bands, having one hell of a good time.

Like most of The Rhythm Kings I spent most of my time in the bar, but I did see the occasional world famous Rock group. The Undertones were great, Wishbone Ash dreadful, The Blues Band played some middle-class blues and the Q-Tips looked good, played badly and went down a storm.

Elvis Costello kept everyone waiting. The backstage area was suddenly cleared, a carpet was fetched to cover the stage, and a hush fell over the assembled throngs as rumours of his impending arrival spread quicker than a plate of Stork margarine in the sun, until finally the clouds parted, the sun bounced out and there he was before us. He played OK.

Afterwards, despite numerous drinks, Sigmund Freud, our driver, and Dangerous Abe Cohen, our apprentice manager at the time, managed to round everyone up, pile them into the van and head off for Noel Redding's place in Clonakilty where we were to stay for the night. On the way we got hopelessly lost, mainly because the Individual was positive he knew the way and kept giving 'advice' and 'directions' for 'short cuts'. We got to the point where if anyone recommended that we went one way, Freud would automatically turn the van around and go the other way. We eventually got there around five in the morning to find Noel Redding waiting for us with tea, bread and butter and volumes of Jimi Hendrix anecdotes. Redding still looks as if stepped straight off the cover of the *Sgt Pepper* album – psychedelic shades, curly hair and eighteenth century military jacket. He runs rehearsal rooms cum guesthouse operation (mainly for bands) in Clonakilty, and his stories and lifestyle are a constant reminder of a way of life most of us only shook hands with, but never really knew.

This is where the magazine piece ends. Then, recently, he wrote:

The Mountain Dew Festival was the only festival with a hotel nearby. That was luxury for us. One of our future drummers, Gonz Houlihan was in the audience and waited until three years ago to join us. **"**

All we were trying to do was promote Macroom

John Martin Fitz-Gerald

Tadhg Kelleher
1982, Salonika

" I am a sound engineer, but I also played as part of Salonika in the last year of the festival. I was with Declan Finnegan, Gerry McCarthy and the late Michael O'Sullivan, playing a little folk, trad, bluegrass and country. We played in the marquee at Coolcower Estate. Jean Yves Marie Tourbin played too and I know him well. He's the most unusual person you'll ever meet – an evangelist from a wealthy background from Brittany. As a sound engineer I have recorded fourteen albums for him.

He was living in Loughitane, Co Kerry, when he played at Macroom. He always used the best musicians and the performance was excellent, inspiring, thought provoking. He still practices what he preaches, embracing all walks of life. He was on after us. We were there early in the morning. It was the first time I had ever bought a new van, a green Datsun Urvan as I had packed up working in the Sound Store, and playing in the marquee was great for us. It was covered, but the floor was grass which we didn't expect. The crowds were not big for Salonika, but they increased as time went on. We weren't as well known as the other acts which followed us, and we knew that. The Chieftains, Clannad and Freddie White were on after us. **"**

Gerry Lane
1979, Driveshaft 1982,
The West Cork Band

" I have been living in Gran Canaria for the last 23 years, still writing and playing music. Thinking about the Macroom Mountain Dew Festival takes me back far to when I did gigs for Martin Fitz-Gerald in The Hooded Cloak when I played with Southern Comfort and Galaxy (with Senator Brian Crowley) as well as Driveshaft.

I went to my first Mountain Dew Festival in 1977 to see Rory Gallagher; I was a huge fan. The atmosphere was electric. Rory took the head off the place! Dónal, his brother, was always behind him and he did a lot for us too. I moved the band to London in 1983 and Dónal was very helpful. A real gentleman.

As part of the West Cork Band I played in the Square with the late Noel Redding (ex-bass player with Jimi Hendrix), Oliver Murphy from Bandon and Brian Calnan on drums. I remember the organisers were keen to make sure there were plenty of free gigs and this was one of them. I'd say we only played for about forty minutes. The Driveshaft gig was different as we were in the marquee which held a huge number. Tadgh Kelleher of Sulán Studios was on sound and it was his first night using a new Bose system. It was impressive with small speakers which had incredible power. The marquee was full and we got a great reaction. Phil Lynott played at the festival that year and we did a tour with him the next year. Denis Desmond managed Phil's next band Grand Slam and us for a few years, so we toured together. He organised for us to release the EP *Live Cutz*. 500 copies were made and I saw that a copy of it sold recently on eBay for €300! I'm sorry I only have one copy. "

Con Downing

143

TJM Tutty

1982, The Atrix

"I was playing bass, and as far as I can recall, the Mountain Dew Festival was my first gig with The Atrix. I had been asked to join the band by John Borrowman, sadly no longer with us, and had done some rehearsals in preparation for the gig. I believe the reason John had asked me to play was that Dick Conroy had left the band and they needed a bass player to fulfill some bookings for the summer. So there I was on stage in Macroom in a large tent in daylight.

I remember getting about halfway into the first or second number in the set when my amplifier stopped working and there was lots of smoke – dead amp! Being on a big stage and with everything miked up and my bass also plugged into the PA, my amp not working did not much affect the sound out front. However, on stage I could not hear what I was playing and did virtually the whole gig without hearing myself, so musically it was a non-event for me. It was sort of weird playing, not hearing oneself, yet the audience probably was not much aware of it. By all accounts, the band sounded fine and apparently I played alright, all things considered.

I cannot remember much else about the festival as we probably had no money to spend on having a good time and, as we were on in the daylight hours, we probably returned to Dublin.

I only played with the band for a few months and they may have broken up soon after that summer.

I still write, play, record and perform mostly for pleasure, and if people see fit to pay me something I am happy for that.

As for the music business, it is the domain of control freaks, gangsters, thieves, and worse. There are, of course, genuine artists and promoters everywhere including in the music business and thankfully I have been privileged to play with, and for, some wonderful people including The Atrix over the decades."

Macroom: The town that never reared a fool

Old saying

Paul Butler
1982 , Neuro

" Thinking about the festival is like opening an old closet, you wouldn't know what you would find in there. Phil Lynott was very good to us and we went on tour with him through 1982. We stayed in Coolcower House which was like a stately home. We felt very privileged. We had done one or some festivals at that stage, an anti-nuclear one at Carnsore Point, another in Lisdoonvarna which had started after the first Macroom one. We did one in Galway with the Boomtown Rats too.

I had already been to the festival to see Rory Gallagher in 1977 with our manager Eoin Ronayne, and both memories of it, as a performer and attending one, were that the whole thing was done very well. I enjoyed it. Everyone was in together, it was a friendly environment and I felt that the Macroom people were enjoying it and glad to have the festival there. It was noticeably friendly. I heard there was some incident of someone trying to get over a fence to get in for nothing, but that happens everywhere. It seemed to have been sorted out quickly. We would be glad if there was another festival in Macroom as I am part of a new band called Propeller Palms. If there is one, I hope we will be invited! "

Shea Morris (AKA Aeon)
1982 , Neuro

" That was a great festival. After we played there on the main stage, we met Philo (Phil Lynott) backstage when we were having a few beers. He had been side of stage watching and liked the look and sound of the band. After that we toured, worked and together in the studio recorded 'While You Were Waiting' which was produced by Philo, but never released. "

Fortune favours the brave and that's what the Macroom festival committee was.

John Creedon 1977/78

Paddy Moloney

1980 & 1982, The Chieftains

" We played at the Mountain Dew twice and each of them was an enjoyable experience. It's always good to meet other musicians. I had recorded a few albums with Mike Oldfield and had spent time in his house. He actually sent a private plane to bring me there, high up in the mountains – an unusual spot. He was on after us in the 1980 Macroom concert and afterwards side-stage he sat down and played my uilleann pipes – he loved them.

I remember the rain at the festival, I think it was the 1982 one. It didn't stop the music, though. I do remember that the 1982 concert was not a success financially and at that stage I felt we were part of the organisation and that their loss was our loss and that we should share the financial burden. I was sorry it had to end.

I continue to tour around the world (despite my current ankle break) and have just composed a piece for my grandson, four-year-old Fionn. It's scored for a symphony orchestra and has African drums, harps, and starts with a heartbeat, building towards a seven-minute lullaby. It's something for him to have for later. "

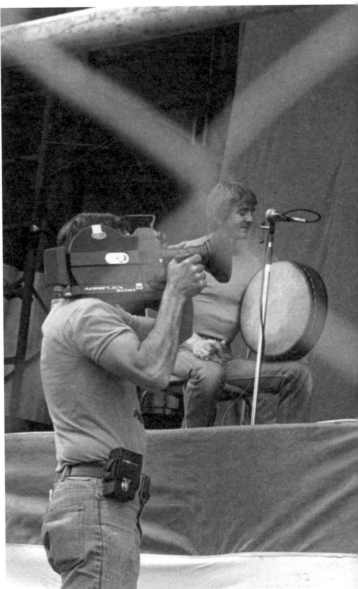

Kevin Conneff, Matt Molloy, Paddy Moloney *Cork Examiner/Evening Echo*

6. Papers and Punters

Opinions varied on the level at which trouble came to Macroom. The media looked for stories, ideally shocking ones to gain front-page headlines. The ingredients were there – big crowds, successful musicians, groupies, fans, people having fun, perhaps facilitated by some 'wacky baccie'. People living in Macroom had their own opinions and plenty to say about their festival.

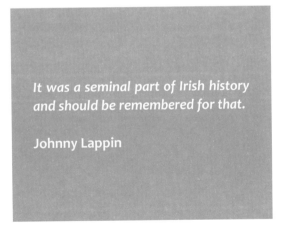

It was a seminal part of Irish history and should be remembered for that.

Johnny Lappin

Con Downing
1976 –1982,
Festival Press Officer, Journalist

"Before I became editor of *The Southern Star* in 2009 I worked part-time writing for the newspaper. I attended the first festival as a music lover and some of the following years acted as a press officer, helping with organising interviews, as well as writing reports for the newspaper.

It was a busy time, but I remember Marianne Faithfull as quite demure, withdrawn even, as she had had a tough time on drugs and was on a comeback tour. She was one of the biggest stars to have ever performed in County Cork and people turned up in their thousands to see her.

When Rory Gallagher played in the second year of the festival, it was the first successful, properly run outdoor concert, unlike in stadiums in Dublin, with more hints of Woodstock than anything else. Elvis Costello didn't endear himself to the audience – no empathy at all. Paul Young was different. He made up for Costello and was very obliging when I organised press interviews. The Atrix was a punk/new wave band and John Barrowman, who since died, was very nice, not at all like his fierce presence on stage. The other Irish bands such as Moving Hearts, Clannad and The

Chieftains were all easy to deal with.

The concerts were moved to Coolcower House for the last two years. It was a good facility, with the house nearby for the acts to relax and change in. The owners, the Casey family, were very hospitable. Before the concerts moved there, the house was used as a location for parties, and the 1978 Hot Press awards were presented there.

I managed Driveshaft at one time and played music myself a bit. I looked after the acts which played in Coolcower, where many of them stayed. Phil Lynott was a hell of a nice guy to deal with. He was wound up and never sat still. But Thin Lizzy fans had no interest in Phil Lynott on his own, and he didn't draw the same crowd as he would have with the original band.

It was a totally mad time for all of us. We were in our early twenties and enjoyed the influx of all the talent. The festival started out very well and perhaps peaked too soon with the Rory concerts. Macroom was a victim of its own success with others emulating it. It was a pace-setter for other festivals which did the ground work for them. By the time it ended, we had a 16% mortgage interest rate. These were tough times, with less to spend on weekends away in Macroom. A great festival had run its course and it was wise to call it a day.

John Sheehan

Jim Carroll

2011, Irish Times, from
'20 Unforgettable Festival Memories'

1: Rory Gallagher, Macroom Mountain Dew festival, 1977. One of the strangest ever yarns from Irish music is that the Macroom Mountain Dew festival organisers invited Idi Amin to town in 1977. The Ugandan dictator didn't show, and punters had to instead make do with a magnificent show from Rory Gallagher, which was a much better result for all concerned. The festival continued and, by 1981, was hosting The Undertones, Elvis Costello, The Pretenders and Paul Brady, and charging £12 for weekend tickets.

> *Elvis Costello was brilliant, world class, and to think he came to Macroom!*
>
> **Bill Hennigan**

John Sheehan

Photographer

I was a stringer with *The Irish Press*, *The Corkman* and *The Southern Star*, so I went to the festival every year. It's something you wouldn't want to miss.

One clear memory is how casual things were. The stars were right there so you felt part of it all. Usually at big concerts you are rushed in at a certain time and rushed out. At Macroom I felt able to wander onto the stage. You wouldn't be able to do that today. Real hot summer days made for interesting shots. I'm disgusted with one incident when I was coming out of Coolcower House. Phil Lynott came over to me and asked me for a lift to the performance area up the fields. I got such a shock I didn't take out the camera. A missed opportunity!

I thought the Lynott concert went very well. Of course I was concentrating on him and on the fans who were right up in front of the stage. They all seemed to be enjoying themselves. One thing clear to me about the organisation of the festival over the years was that the committee rolled up their sleeves and if there was a problem they just got on and solved it. I really admired them for that.

Hermann Hemp
Photographer

"Rory Gallagher was in Cork City Hall at a time when I took photographs for Con Downing of *The Southern Star*. I met Rory afterwards and talked about hurling when he would stand behind the goalposts watching his team, so I knew him before I took photographs of him in Macroom. I saw Johnny Rotten at the Mountain Dew Festival and he really lived up to his name.

We had all got used to good music in West Cork where I live, due to Connolly's in Leap having terrific musicians to play there. I liked reggae at the time and The Cimarons at the Mountain Dew Festival gave me my first experience of seeing dreadlocks. They were a fantastic sight. People went nuts when they took off their hats and the hair poured out of their colourful hats.

Con Downing was working at the festival and I went along with him for the ride. There was booze and food in abundance, and you couldn't breathe for hash. Everyone seemed to be using it! The music was loud and it took a few days for my hearing to come back."

Lynn Geldof
1978, Young Tribune

"Night-time, blue and orange tents could be seen rising up the sloping side of the campsite overlooking the Lee. Downtown, a 'Bailey' procedure had been adopted against the hordes: pubs closed their doors early, letting in people they deemed acceptable and in measured numbers.

Morning came late to Macroom on Saturday, breakfast identified by the 1pm coils of smoke from aromatic roll-ups were wafting under the nose, Bisto fashion. Youngsters hung around the stage area, expectantly watching the Rock machine being set up. Roadies and managers swaggered. Groups and couples staked out their territory for the day.

On the sidelines the Samaritans' caravan offered assistance to the distressed

Rocky de Valera and his Rhythm Kings blasted open the weekend. I loved the John Wayne song. "Is it a bird, is it a plane? No. it's John Wayne.""

Larry Lyons
1977, Cork Examiner

"Macroom", said the old man in the town Square, "will never be the same again. Even the Redemptorists could not boast of anything like it during the General Mission in my boyhood days". And one of the eight-and-a-half thousand jean brigade looked at him and asked his companion, "is he for real?" "The generation gap", observed a journalist colleague.

I do not pretend to be competent to give a verdict on the Gallagher performance, but my own particular and very personal verdict is that it was a deafening success, and if anyone disagreed with me, I can honestly plead that I cannot hear a word he says.

I found the music weird and wild and unwillingly I found it spellbinding. The audience was good humoured and during the concert there was no trace of viciousness.

And a good time was had by all, although after the Saturday night many were so broke that they had not the £2.50 for Rory's concert. But they lolled in the sun in the Square and heard it if they did not see it.

Isabel Conway
1977 , Cork Examiner

Field Marshall Amin will obviously be flattered by their attentions since he expressed disappointment in a newspaper interview some time ago at not receiving an invitation to Ireland from the Government. When asked if the visit could pose problems for the State, a spokesman for the Department of Foreign Affairs said last evening that it was not unusual for foreign heads of state to make private visits to countries and it did not necessarily involve them. The usual courtesies would, of course, be extended to President Amin if the paid a visit to Ireland, he added.

An annual Rock event unsurpassed in Ireland, and which has brought a spark to the life of Rock music in this country.

Donal Buckley

John Creedon
1977 & 1978, RTÉ

"I was at both of Rory Gallagher's festival concerts. Anywhere Rory was playing, I was there. I was about thirteen years younger than him and he was on a pedestal for me. He was a huge icon, and we were neighbours. He lived with his family off Patrick's Hill and my family lived at the bottom of it at Inchigeela Dairy. His mother was a regular in our shop and she and my mother were great friends. In fact, my sister Geraldine created the sculpture to commemorate Rory that stands on Rory Gallagher Plaza at Paul Street in Cork.

It was interesting how Rory had gone over the wall in denim, accepted and appreciated by the establishment. It was quite a political time. I had three button badges then: 'Free Nelson Mandela', 'Steve Biko Lives' and 'CND'. We were mad as Hell! It was cool to be politically aware, as perhaps it is now since the last referendum which got people motivated.

At the time of the Mountain Dew Festival the Northern Troubles were at their height and a lot of fans came down for Rory's concerts. I remember the sloping field where the concert was held, long before we ever heard the term 'natural amphitheatre'. The festival must have inspired many others too.

It came to mind as I thought about the festival that the style of the time never really went out – desert boots, the sea of denim, woolly hats and jumpers. Hairdressing wasn't the same standard that it is now, though! Still, it was boys meet girls, add music and stir – you have a great time.

Fortune favours the brave and that's what the Macroom festival committee was."

And to think this all happened because of Macroom!

*Mike Lowe to
Dónal Gallagher after 1977*

Anne Sweeney

1978 , The Longford Leader

" Jenny Haan: A graceful and provocative leap onto the stage, dressed completely in virgin white, followed by her Yorkshire based band, Lion, the five boys from Dublin were quickly forgotten about. Five foot nothing Jenny was a petite bundle of power and sexuality with a voice to match. Her performance was electro-dynamic, truly volatile. She danced in white ballet slippers at times delicate and looking quite fragile; often provocatively twisting her waist-length hair in tantalising movements around her; but always with style. Her voice was raunchy, her band heavy and they made everybody stand up. Talking to her afterwards she said her mother was a ballet dancer which accounts for her ability to dance so well.

Then reggae music filled the air. It was The Cimarons, five boys with colourful woollen caps and scarves. The crowd loved them, and they got everybody relaxed. The bass player jumped around the stage with a bottle of Johnson's baby lotion in his mouth and the lead singer shrugged his shoulders up and down as he bopped time to the music. They played longer than anyone, and even though the rain poured from the heavens the crowd cheered and clapped and wouldn't let them off. Towards the end of their set they discarded their caps, revealing dark plaited hair.

One 56-year-old Dublin lady clutched a giant poster of Rory Gallagher and looked very much at home. She had come with her 16-year-old son to see the Cork superstar and was very annoyed that one hawker had asked her, "What the hell are you doing here?" Gallagher put all he had into the 90 minutes and loved it even more than the crowd. For the first 20 minutes he went through old favourites like 'Tattoo Lady' and then his back-up men left him and he played on an acoustic guitar. The boys returned and they went straight into 'Bought and Sold' which made the crowd ecstatic.

The power and energy from that small man behind his guitar is amazing. He played it bending around the supporting poles, standing on a chair and jumping in the air. Unobserved by the crowd, his mother stood in the corner of the press enclosure and cheered and clapped and rocked as much as his fans. At the end of his act Rory was sweating and his shirt was saturated but the crowd wanted more and for four minutes they clapped and shouted. He returned and performed two encores. Gallagher left, as he arrived, in a huge brown car down a narrow laneway at the back of the stage. "

Denis Minihane

Photographer, Cork Examiner
& Evening Echo

"I covered a lot of the festivals over the years for *The Cork Examiner* and *Evening Echo*, and there was always a great buzz there. It was always good fun to cover it. Rory was easy to get a good action shot of – he was pretty lively and people loved him and were easy to photograph too. I remember those years as always being bright and sunny with people wearing short sleeves and lounging around on the grass around the Castle. It was a great assignment to go to."

Eddie O'Hare

Photographer, Cork Examiner
& Evening Echo

"I worked at quite a few of the festivals and went off my own bat too for a few of them. I loved getting pics backstage. I was young, agile and energetic and brazen too, and would do anything for a good pic. I had a good relationship with a lot of the stars and their management, so they often let me stay. The rule was that you would be allowed to take pics during three consecutive songs and then you had to go and make room for someone else. I knew the score from taking pics of Michael Jackson in Wembley before he came to Cork, and of Queen, The Rolling Stones, Dylan, Springsteen.

In the first few years of concerts there weren't so many photographers jostling for good pics, but in latter years we have been herded like cattle and the three song rule is applied more stringently. I was assaulted by heavies at David Bowie's Slane concert. They didn't want pics of Bowie to be taken and pulled the film out of my camera. It was all very violent and I made the front page of all the newspapers and was interviewed by Pat Kenny.

I was always trying to get atmospheric pics of Cork people at concerts outside Cork and I was hoisted up on someone's shoulders for some of the published pics at the Mountain Dew Festival. I remember climbing up on scaffolding and being told to get down, which I did, but not until I got the pic I wanted. I was always looking for something quirky. I got a few good pics of Van Morrison that time. I got to know Joe O'Herlihy who was always obliging for pics of U2 after that."

Niall Stokes

*2009. Interviewed by Michael Carr
in The Irish Examiner*

"We were all aware that this was a ground-breaking event. Everyone involved in *Hot Press* drove down. One of the memories I have is of the entrepreneurship that sprang up around the festival. You couldn't bring bottles into the concert, for instance, so someone had set up a stall near the entrance, where you could buy a bucket to put your drink in.

I remember the excitement that greeted Gallagher's arrival in an Aston Martin. Rory had a straw cowboy hat on. He bounded on to the stage, and from the moment he struck his first chord, the atmosphere was just electric. People like The Edge were there. It was part of what inspired him to become a musician. You had a whole wave of bands that came along, after that, who were inspired by Rory, Van Morrison and Thin Lizzy. There was a sense that if they could do it, then other bands could too.

It was a watershed, a moment which more than any other marked the changing of the guard. Rory Gallagher was invited back to headline the festival in 1978, and in the same year The Police headlined Ireland's second outdoor Rock festival at Leixlip in Co Kildare. Macroom had pioneered something that began to spread, and before long Dublin had its own version at Dalymount Park. Meanwhile, the crowds kept flocking to Macroom."

Alf McCarthy

1978

"I hadn't started working in RTÉ at that stage, but if Rory was playing it was always special and worth going to wherever he was. My clear memory is of bringing my first-born daughter Ruthie to the concert as a toddler and enjoying her dancing to Rory's music. She loved it! She married a bass player, so who knows how strong that influence was! Rory was not just special as a talent, but as a really nice guy. He hated the trappings of the industry and that kept him real. I think that what we saw was someone who related to all of us and we felt huge pride in his talent.

I was a regular at Shanley's pub in Clonakilty and remember meeting The Blues Band's Tom McGuinness there with Noel Redding and did interviews with them over the years. I look back on Macroom with great affection and appreciation of what was achieved there."

Donal Buckley
1978, Irish Independent (extracts)

" The back-up groups and singers who led the concert had the unenviable task of entertaining the crowd and in some cases suffered humiliation of playing to an unmoved audience who did little more than tolerate their presence.

Not that the groups weren't good, in fact, with the line-up of Jenny Haan's Lion (who gave an incredible performance), Hot Guitars, Stepaside, The Cimarons and Joe O'Donnell and his Vision Band, they could hardly have been better. Each of these groups would, in their own right, deserve star billing at a lesser event, but pitched against the backdrop of a man like Gallagher, they were just not in his league.

One notable exception, though, were The Cimarons who with their percussive reggae sound set a scintillating musical pace that only Gallagher was to surpass.

Speaking to Rory afterwards in the comfortable surrounds of the pavilion of Macroom Golf Club (his retreat from the fans) it was strange to see him without his guitar. It was like looking at Jack Lynch without his pipe or Shirley Bassey minus her eyelashes.

"I had never thought the original line-up would last more than six months and to think it lasted seven years, that says something." Why then retain Gerry McEvoy? "Gerry and I have always had a great relationship on stage. His playing inspires me. I don't know, it's something that's difficult to explain, but when you're playing with someone like Gerry, you get a special kind of spark, besides, he's a great bass player."

As far as the media in general is concerned, Gallagher remains something of an enigma. This is probably due to the fact the he doesn't like to 'flirt with the press', as he puts it, which in turn, is probably why he often gets the thin edge of the reporter's pen. "I don't think the press have treated me fairly", says Rory. "If things are going badly, they delight in knocking you, and if they are going well, they think they should be going better."

In the Mountain Dew Festival we are assured of an annual Rock event unsurpassed in Ireland, and which has brought a spark to the life of Rock music in this country. "

Seán Keane, Martin Fay and Derek Bell of The Chieftains
Cork Examiner/Evening Echo

Pat Lynch
1978, *The Kerryman/The Corkman*

" Jackets studded with iron or brass or copper rubbed shoulders with plastic or real leather. Red trousers were stuffed into oversized riding boots without spurs, bottom-flared slacks showing beneath ill-fitting anoraks that were topped by Stetson hats or bargees' caps with high crowns and small peaks.

Most carried rolls of bedding which many threw on the sidewalks as sitting pads or lounging beds from which they observed the passing scene as they drank stout or beer or coke from bottles in six-packs or pint glasses brought from pubs that presented closed doors to the streets. "

Dick Hogan
1978, *Irish Times*

" It started to rain as the last intense strains of Joe O'Donnell's electric fiddle began to ship his band into a spiralling finale. Gallagher was next. "Welcome to Macroom", he said. "Welcome yourself", someone behind me said.

The rain lightened to a drizzle and, on cue, a rainbow arched over the field. Gallagher turned, nodded to his band and the place was alight with movement. Pubs on Main Street, bar only the brave, locked up with cash registers and Rory Gallagher still ringing in their ears. "

The marquee at Coolcower
Cork Examiner/Evening Echo

Marcus Connaughton
1978, RTÉ

" One thing that stood out about the Macroom Mountain Dew Festival was the access people had to the performers. You could go up and talk to most of them. I remember Joe O'Donnell in 1978. At that time no-one in Ireland was giving Irish tunes a Rock accompaniment – it was usually something done in America – so it was good to see one of our own doing it. And of course Rory Gallagher was one of our own.

The atmosphere was incredible on the day Rory played. It seemed brilliantly organised and we thought the stage remarkable. It was a huge development within Irish culture. There was a kind of community of musicians – a bit avant garde and everyone knew everyone else. And it was special because it was the first open-air festival in Ireland. There had been attempts under canvas which were pretty poor.

In 1977 the sun shone and the buzz was just electrifying. We had a very, very good time and the gig was powerful. It had a lovely naivety which we all had at the time, a harmlessness. Bad suits and hairdos perhaps, but there was no aggression, no binge drinking, no shots. You set out to enjoy yourself, and drink was a side product. And no mobile phones! Macroom worked – being contained in the Castle grounds was a good idea. Macroom lit the flame and got other festivals going. "

Vincent Power
1978, Irish Weekly Examiner

" The Cimarons were one of the pillars of the British reggae scene and had Carl Levy on keyboards, Franklyn Dunn on bass, Locksley Giche on drums, Maurice Ellis on drums and Winston Reid (Reedy) on vocals.

Joe O'Donnell, there with his Vision Band, had once played his violin with Granny's Intentions, East of Eden and Headstone. Here his band comprised of Dave Lennos, keyboards, Theodore Thunder on drums and Wilf Smith on bass. "

Without a doubt it was the biggest thing to ever hit Macroom.

Margaret Linehan

Dermot Russell

1978, Irish Examiner

"There were plenty of quick fire speeches from the platform in the town square, culminating in rapid repartee from television entertainer, Mike Murphy. The throng relished every bit of the talk, the politicians even avoided vote-catching speeches and everything went according to plan. But the value of the festival was there in the background. The solid knowledge that between now and the finish on Sunday week 90,000 people will visit Macroom for the various festival highlights was there as an accepted fact. Not to mention the assumption that these visitors will leave about a million pounds behind them.

Festival President Denis Murphy, a local businessman, had fine words for the crowd which assembled for the opening ceremony and to watch the industrial parade which preceded it. So had Chairman Pat O'Connell and the brown eyed Marjorie Corcoran, an unlikely but a most efficient Chairman of the Macroom Urban District Council, charm and good looks she wears naturally.

Kevin Jer O'Sullivan spoke well on behalf of one of the major festival sponsors, Murphy's Brewery, and so did Joe Maguire, representing the other major sponsors, Gaeltarra Eireann.

In Rory we have a Rock musician of world stature, something rare in this country, and in the Mountain Dew Festival we are assured of an annual Rock event surpassed in Ireland and which has brought a long-awaited spark to the life of Rock music in this country."

Denis Reading

1978, Irish Examiner

"Johnny Rotten, the controversial ex lead singer with the Sex Pistols group, got a truly rotten reception at the concert. Members of the festival committee were annoyed to hear that a presentation was to be made to the singer and at the festival one of the committee members, Michael Lynch, said that as stage organiser, he was not going to allow Rotten onto the stage. "No way would we have Johnny Rotten on stage. We don't want Punk Rock. We are Rock. As you can see from the crowd gathered here today, they are all very well behaved. You could take them anywhere, they are a good crowd. I am sure that parents would not want their children at a Punk Rock festival".

The camera-shy Johnny Rotten, wearing a long black coat, blue suede shoes and who had brown elastic bands in his hair, said that he did not want to go on stage anyway."

Maurice Gubbins

1979, Irish Examiner

" Basking in the blazing sun in a Macroom field, eating sandwiches and enjoying live folk music. What a way to spend a Sunday afternoon!

Top of the bill at the grounds this year were the Furey Brothers and Davey Arthur, who more than lived up to their growing reputation and they managed to get everybody singing, and quite a few performing jigs and reels of various descriptions. Their rendering of the anti-war song 'Green Fields of France' was particularly memorable. Probably the biggest hit of the day was Donegal-man Paul Brady who left them screaming for more, even after his encore. As always, his classic version of 'Arthur McBride' was superb.

Jim McCann and his group, which includes Corkman Matthew Manning, were first on stage and they provided a pleasing opening to the proceedings. Ronnie Drew had to be hoisted on stage because of a leg injury and Donnacha Ó Dulaing performed a marathon chat session to keep the crowd on the boil until The Dubliners launched into a set which began with 'Fermoy Lassies'. Green-clad duo Foster and Allen were late replacements at yesterday's "
concert.

Tony O'Brien

1981, Irish Independent

"Loud Rock music and nearly 10,000 dedicated fans helped swell the funds of a boys' club and the local Girl Guides in Macroom, Co Cork, at the weekend. Paying £12 for a weekend ticket, the huge crowd endured nearly 15 hours of Rock music during the fifth Macroom Music Festival. And in the two days, Gardaí made only a handful of arrests for minor drug offences and petty larceny.

As the crowd enjoyed an international line-up which included top British acts Elvis Costello and the Attractions, The Blues Band as well as leading Irish bands, they were adding to the funds of two local charities.

The two-day Rock event – which cost more than £60,000 to stage – came as the culmination of the week long fifth Macroom Mountain Dew Festival.

Money raised from the festival goes to local charities and this year it is the turn of Macroom Boys Club and Girl Guides. About £2,000 will be raised from the festival.

Gardaí patrolled the site but kept a low profile and stewarding was left to 150 specially-employed security men.

The Rock festival opened on Saturday afternoon on a site leased from a local family about a mile from Macroom town.

Under an indifferent sky a crowd of more than 8,000 reacted listlessly to the music blasting at them from a 15,000 watt sound system until the arrival of The Blues Band just before 7 o'clock.

The band, led by ex-Manfred Mann pop idol Paul Jones, had the crowd shouting for more with a blistering delivery of blues standards in the same way they lifted last year's Lisdoonvarna festival out of the doldrums. "

It was my first time going to a gig. All the best musicians were playing that day with Rory Gallagher. He was an incredible influence on me as a guitar player, particularly early on.

The Edge 1977

Anne Ryan

1981, The Corkman

"The Rhythm Kings started the concert moving about 2.00 that afternoon. These are a new up and coming group, with lead singer Ferdia MacAnna. He is in the tradition of Bob Geldof and is a journalist turned singer who wrote some of his own lyrics. The Rhythm Kings should really be pleased with themselves because they made the splash they wanted to. Sniff 'n' the Tears were nothing to cry over, they were just one great big smile. Their clear pure soulful Heavy Metal/Rock grabbed the crowd who swayed ecstatically, especially as they climaxed in the last two numbers.

The Blues Band were tops. Lead singer, Paul Jones, sang one song that summed up their performance too. That was when he sang about special relationships and shouted to the crowd there is another special relationship too, that between a crowd and the audience. This was during the song, 'Treat Your Woman Right'.

Unassuming, straightforward musician, Paul Brady, trying hard to make it for the last couple of years, comes across as a dedicated man. His return visit to Macroom this year was much more rewarding than last year. Then, he was upstaged by groups of people breaking through the fences. His true voice, reminiscent of Van Morrison at times, kept the youth quietly entranced. Until his recent hit, 'Crazy Dreams', when the mob, like the words of his final song, 'bust loose'.

Scullion and Q-Tips gave a good performance too."

John Vaughan

Macroom

"My claim to fame is that I drove Rory Gallagher from the concert in 1978 to Coolcower for the Hot Press awards. I was friends with the Chairman Denis Murphy – we often worked together at the Palace Cinema – and in various theatrical productions, so he got me involved to work on security and other jobs like looking after what we considered to be 'offensive weapons' like equipment used to erect tents and so on. I drove Maurice Cullen's car so that Rory would not be mobbed and we had a lovely, relaxed chat as we went along. We just talked about the gig and things in general. He was very unassuming. I worked at most of the concerts in some capacity or other and they were good times."

Michael O'Connell,
1977, 1980 & 1982

" I went to a lot of festivals in those days and they all seem to meld into one. What I remember is that the Castle grounds were an ideal amphitheatre for the concerts and that I enjoyed them all.

I remember sitting on the grass on a nice day. I had seen Rory Gallagher tons of times and he was as good as ever; undoubtedly he was a brilliant guitarist. He seemed less innovative than in his Taste days, but I remember enjoying it.

Van Morrison was grumpy as usual, partly because the crowds were quite boisterous, shouting the songs they wanted played and he never responds well to that. The music was still good. I wasn't overly committed to Phil Lynott as I had seen Thin Lizzy in the City Hall in Cork and come out with my ears nearly bleeding. It was a relief that the sound was dissipated in the open-air. I have been to the Isle of Wight festival where there were good stands for food and perhaps the facilities were better, but Macroom was nonetheless enjoyable. Macroom was more like the Lisdoonvarna festival and I don't remember any trouble in any of the years. I remember seeing the drug squad around as I recognised them from my time representing some of the

offenders in court. When I was in Macroom district court later in the year of one of the festivals, I remember some prosecutions for drug offences, but there were very few relative to the number that attended. "

Gonz Houlihan
1980

"I remember it being the first day of the two-day festival in Macroom in 1981. Elvis Costello and The Attractions and The Undertones were the head-liners as well as The Blues Band. I was a big fan of The Undertones and I liked Elvis Costello too but I was mainly there for The Undertones.

While we were there in this field having a beer or whatever, this band comes out, The Rhythm Kings, with a singer called Rocky de Valera. I remember being hooked straight away on this sound. They seemed to have a bit of everything – showband, punk, Rock 'n' Roll, the Ramones hits: the dancehall sort of thing. I thought to myself, now that's the sort of band I'd love to play with. I was starting out on drums at the time so the name Rhythm Kings sounded even better to me. I remember waking up in a Hare Krishna tent having been given veg and boiling water in a cup. We continued to rock out to Paul Brady and more that day.

It was my first real outdoor Rock festival gig and I'd discovered a new Irish band for myself – The Rhythm Kings – and I continued to go see them at different events still thinking how cool to play in a band like them. They broke up and the years passed and thirty years later I'm browsing Facebook and I see a post on Pat O'Mahony's page: Rocky de Valera and The Rhythm Kings were looking for a drummer. I had nothing to lose, and if I got an audition at least I could say I played with them for a few songs. So off I went in and blasted out three numbers. I knew I had done ok, and two hours or so later I got the call "Do you want the gig? It's yours!" I was on the Luas with my wife at the time of the call. It was a great feeling, as good as being asked by The Stones.

So in 2012 I finally got to play with the band that was huge influence on me 30 years later. They were all truly great guys and fun to hang out and play with and still are. And it all started over 30 years ago in Macroom and I'm grateful for that.

Harry Morrison
1980

I had heard Mike Oldfield would be playing a rare full concert of *Tubular Bells*. He had only ever played it twice up to that time, so that was a big one for me. He brought musicians to play all the instruments. There weren't many fancy lights as there would usually be, but Maggie Reilly of Stagalee was on vocals and did a lot with him. I don't think his sister Sally was with him that time. I don't remember who the other musicians were, but I remember being impressed. They were the cream of the crop at that time, and they were amazing.

The whole line-up of the day was impressive. I'm still a fan of Van Morrison and had met him some years back. He had a massive band with him, including two drummers. He did a full set, including my favourite song from the album *Common One*, 'Summertime in England'. The audience was responsive. It was a huge coup to have got him there. Paul Brady is always good and was this day too.

I noticed that Mike Oldfield was side-stage for The Chieftains set and was listening and applauding. Lindisfarne were billed last and the skies opened up after a few songs and they lost most of their audience, including myself.

It was the first open-air concert of that size in Ireland. There were Hare Krishnas going up and down the street, banging their drums and ringing their bells. They turned up at any big event in those times and had arrived from Dublin, Galway, and Kerry. You could get a free vegetarian meal from them down the town, with free indoctrination thrown in. For the rest of us, a field for our tent, plenty of pubs and good music was all we needed.

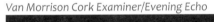

Van Morrison Cork Examiner/Evening Echo

Tony Hegarty
1980, 1981 & 1982

"" I went to many festivals and I was a teacher in Macroom for a while so was well aware of the Mountain Dew Festival.

I remember that for Van Morrison it was a really sunny day, and while he was his usual grumpy self, he gave his usual good performance, particularly of 'Cleaning Windows'. For me Lindisfarne were the highlight. They really got the crowd going. 'Fog on the Tyne' is a song I used to play with my brother Owen as they were popular in the early seventies. The mandolin playing was really good. The Undertones in '81, ordinary lads from Derry, appealed to the younger set. They had had one album which had 'Teenage Kicks' on it, and a lot of people knew the songs.

Moving Hearts in '82 were popular with a certain audience; Christy Moore was political at that time. You could see the real fans up at the top near the stage for all the concerts, then there would be others floating at the back, not taking much notice of the talent on the stage. That's how it is at all festivals. The town was grand, no hint of hassle. A lot of people hitched there. It was all quite innocent. ""

Valerie Dineen

" I was in my early teens at the time of the first few festivals and there was pressure on for me to study instead of staying out late and going to concerts. I wasn't really fussed about Marianne Faithfull as she appealed to an older age group, but I did go to see her and I just remember how hot it was in The Dome. My memories are more concentrated on the buzz and commotion of the festival.

I thought it odd that shops were boarded up, but at the same time I could see that music and something exciting was going on. There was a lot of noise and buzz in the town leading-up to the festival. I have a clear memory of a loudspeaker attached to a pole close to TP Cotter's pub and hearing Olivia Newton John singing 'Totally Devoted to You'. Every time I hear that song it reminds me of the festival.

I remember being interviewed in the Oak Room which was the festival club. I was chatting away and of course I hadn't a clue that it would end up in a newspaper and that I wasn't supposed to have been there at my age. I wasn't drinking, but I should have been at home studying. I remember going home at about 3am and the weather was so good it was very bright. Even if I got away with sneaking into my room at home, someone would always spot me going

home. Macroom is a small place!

I helped out very little really, but I was able to get backstage for the Rory Gallagher concert and into the golf club which was a great privilege. I flew to London one time and who sat beside me but Dónal Gallagher and we spoke about our links to the festival. My husband Kevin was and is a great Rory fan and we even diverted to St Oliver's cemetery one day to see Rory's grave.

The main thing is that it was a music festival and we enjoyed all sorts. I thought The Cimarons were very colourful and fun. I remember lovely weather, no need for wellies, and debris in one of the tents in the Castle grounds. All the signs of a good time. "

totally different life here than in the city. We were all about farming, hunting and fishing, though I worked in Cork. If any of them misbehaved they were lined up and given a severe talking to by the Gardaí.

They were happy, simple years, people having a good time. We knew how to enjoy ourselves, people were relaxed and talked to strangers. Martin Fitz-Gerald and the other organisers did a great job to get this festival to Macroom for us.

John Purcell

The festival really put Macroom on the map. I live just outside Macroom at Cooleyhane in farmland on a hill and we could hear the music of the festival from our house. Cars were parked all the way up to our avenue gate. We could smell the drugs, but there was no aggression.

I remember being in the Castle grounds and one of the bands playing Old McDonald's Farm and people going wild for it. We all sang along. I was in the middle of it all, usually a bit better of the drink, some which I brewed myself at home. We had our own Mountain Dew.

Busloads came out from Cork. They really thought we were in the sticks. It was a

Richard Neville

I went to the Van Morrison concert. I came in from the Raleigh side of town, using the same entrance as Van Morrison. I followed him in, and a Garda I knew spotted me. You'd know all the gardaí in those days. He called me over, so I got in free.

There was great excitement in the town. In 1980 it was my first outdoor concert. As I followed him, Van Morrison was a sour divil. He made no remarks, just played, but he played well and people obviously enjoyed him. I couldn't complain about any sour puss when I had got in for nothing!

Joe Cohen

1978

"I was Secretary of the Northern Ireland Guitar Society which lasted for about six years. We used to have about 100 members who played all genres of guitar music. We filled a minibus and went to the Mountain Dew Festival to hear Rory. John Flanagan was our driver and we camped near the Castle grounds.

Rory asked me to stay for the presentation to him by *Hot Press* for his *Against the Grain* album. You can see me saying "congratulations, Rory" on the German documentary. I get a great kick out of being able to say that! I remember the awards ceremony and Rory and his brother Dónal being uneasy with Bob Geldof and Johnny Rotten. It was then that I spoke to Rory about becoming president of our society. "What would I need to do?" he asked. He was nervous about me asking him questions about musical theory if he came to give a seminar as part of his presidency. I told him I didn't read music.

I remember speaking to Rory's mum and I asked her if she liked her son's music. "I love it!" she said. "*Shadow Play* is my favourite." I got a great kick when I shuffled my way down to the front to Rory's left as he was saying hello to people who came from around the country. He was looking straight at me when he welcomed people from Belfast. I was a fan since Rory came into Crimbles, the record shop where I worked. I got to know Jim Aiken too and he and Rory's brother Dónal would allow me to go backstage. I still ask myself "did this happen to me?"

I rescued a mandolin that someone was about to throw out and I showed it to Rory at one of his concerts. He played it backstage, and honestly I haven't touched it since. I couldn't let anyone touch it after him!"

Macroom lit the flame and got other festivals going.

Marcus Connaughton, 1978

Rory Gallagher Band Cork Examiner/Evening Echo

Dermot Dwyer

1976-1982, Garda Drug Squad

" The drug scene was only developing during the time of the Macroom festival. Macroom people were taken aback when they saw the scruffy lot of unhealthy looking people arriving from the highways and byeways. We had seen hippies before, but not in that quantity.

They arrived in painted wagons and vans of all types and in different stages of disrepair. They brought a lot of dogs with them! The hippies and the music fans were fairly well behaved. Drug users are not usually aggressive, but the dealers are, and that was who we were after. People talk about how there is no harm in a little hash or magic mushrooms, but I have studied the health repercussions of them, and there is plenty of harm.

We charged one guy, a bad one who was dealing a lot in cannabis, LSD and barbiturates, and we knew he was a heavy hitter. He gave his name as John Doe which of course we knew was false, along with an address which was found not to exist. We remanded him in custody and the next day he appeared in Macroom court and I gave evidence against him. The judge said he was entitled to bail. He seemed to want to appear liberal. We found out later that John Doe was wanted in several countries.

I was trying to appeal to common sense. In those days I didn't get frustrated, as I wouldn't let myself. The original hippies were intelligent and had decided to opt out of the rat race and were looking up at the sky. A few years later others arrived and they couldn't even spell. They were never 'in' to opt 'out'! They felt they were hippies, but went into houses that people left behind when they upgraded, as the country was getting more prosperous. They brought bad habits to West Cork. They wanted the hippie life, and the good life at the same time, so they dealt in drugs to sustain their lifestyle.

During the festival, particularly as the years went on, drug dealers came from Dublin to Macroom so we got help from the Dublin drug squad. What really irked me one night was seeing a group of eight sitting on the cenotaph smoking joints. One of them stood up and urinated against it. Pat Carey who started the Cork drug squad with me said we couldn't tolerate that disrespect, so I shone my torch on the text to get them to read it. I said: "They died for Ireland and here you are smoking dope and piddling on their memorial". Two of them in unison replied: "It's eejits they were!"

All in all at the festival, the people smoking dope were pacifists not looking for trouble. They smoked it openly in the Castle grounds, and that and the music was conducive to getting 'high'. We made 80 seizures one day in 1981, but on the busiest days, if there were 100 users and some dealers out of 20,000 who attended, it was a small percentage. The reason we were there was to catch the dealers. We could not stand by and watch them coming in and selling drugs. We owed it to the State not to let it get out of hand.

We were handicapped due to lack of facilities for detaining people, and we had no mobile phones in those day, nor computers. I loved the entrepreneurial spirit of one man who came from Cork. He could see that the toilet facilities were lacking, so he got a partition, perhaps a piece of plywood, and a bucket, and would take anyone aside who wanted to use the bucket and protected their modesty by putting the partition in front of them. He charged then all for it and was kept going all day. I'd say it was about 10p to use it! 🙶🙶

Cork Examiner/Evening Echo

Pat Egan
1977, The Sound Cellar

" I was operating my record shop in Dublin in 1977. I ran a number of buses, three in total, from Dublin. One of them broke down in Fermoy. We were a few hours late arriving in Macroom. I was so out of it, I spent the afternoon in the bar when Rory was on stage. Our buses were so old they did not go much over 20 miles per hour. The journey down took about seven hours and it took us all night to get back to Dublin. "

Evelyn Casey
Coolcower House

" I still have the visitor's book from those years and see that we had a lot of press people staying, as well as some of the stars. In 1978 Lynn Geldof, Bob's sister, was in the book as working for *The Sunday Tribune*. There was BP Fallon, Dave Fanning, quite a few people from RTÉ and print journalists from around the country, including Con Downing, now editor of *The Southern Star*, who organised press interviews here. In 1982 we had The Duskeys who were performing in The Dome, and I remember Dave Duffy, who stars now as Leo in *Fair City*, with his

partner the late Áine O'Connor who was a journalist at the time reporting for RTÉ on the festival. There were quite a few concert promoters too, but their names didn't mean much to me and still don't.

I was so busy serving them all that I hardly noticed who they were or if they were famous. I do remember that fellah with the big black fuzzy hair – Phil Lynott – around the place. People would generally come for a drink and want snacks, and some of them had full meals. And of course many of them stayed here. We had a full house at all times throughout the years.

I was disappointed when the committee decided to call it a day. They had been well organised. They sold the tickets well, had a team collecting rubbish constantly and managed it all. They were all mad, but we knew that, behind it all, they knew what they were doing. It was very exciting at the time for me, and for many it opened up the idea of going to other outdoor concerts. I went to others after that. It was a new era. I admired the directors who put the money up front. "

Don Buckley
Castle Hotel

"I was about 17 at the time of the first festival and my father and mother were running the hotel. I remember that we had to have bouncers on the door as it was so busy. We had to operate a system, allowing a few in when a few left. On Fridays when the backpackers arrived you'd see them all – we called them The Woolies and The Hairies – and of course when Rory Gallagher was playing people didn't know what to expect of the big crowds.

I remember my father frightened the life out of me and I was glad we had our own security. In fact, we had no cause for worry, and while it was a busy time, it wasn't difficult and was very enjoyable. My main memory of the Marianne Faithfull gig is that I was trying to get off with a girl, and was doing well until I went to the toilets and came back and she was gone! I'm sure Marianne was great, but that was my focus.

I particularly enjoyed Freddie White, but for me at my young age, the buzz was all about the crowds which I missed a bit when the main acts moved to Coolcower. My brother Declan was the graphic designer of the Rory Gallagher poster – and other posters – of the festival. "

Mary Pawle

"What an interesting project the Mountain Dew Festival was, and amazing to realise that it started forty years ago! We were living in Kenmare by then and had heard plenty about it, but as it was the time of pregnancy and small babies we didn't venture over there until 1982.

At the Coolcower House venue we were guests of TJM Tutty who was standing in on bass with The Atrix. TJM had been playing bass with Dr Strangely Strange for a number of years.

The headline act was Phil Lynott. Ivan (my husband) remembers the line-up of the band as Darren Wharton, Jerome Rimson and Robbie Brennan. Jerome was from Detroit and a former Motown bass player and had been living in Ireland for some time. He produced the recordings that Dr Strangely Strange did for Tim Booth's animated film *The Prisoner* around that time. Jerome still lives in Ireland and gigs regularly with people such as Karen Underwood. We joined them for a drink and headed home quite early. I think that was the last time that we saw Philip, whom Ivan knew quite well in the very early days in Dublin. It all seems so very long ago but every time that I drive the road past Coolcower House, I think of that day. "

Jack Cotter

"I have a bar on Main Street, as my father and grandfather did for over 120 years. We were so busy that I only got to see Rory Gallagher for about five minutes. I was lucky that Paul Brady came to us every year he played at the festival, and I gave him posters to take away with him. I'm sorry I don't have a photograph of him and my father in the back. I do have the original cut-out of Rory which was on the Castle gates for his concert.

For the last four years we have had a Rory celebration when a tribute band comes to play in our garden at the back. We have links with the Cork Rocks for Rory committee. It's usually held on the second Sunday in June. We have the music and do burgers and generally celebrate Rory's life and music.

I look back on the festival as a fun time. People were no bother. For the volume of people who came from all over the country, we had no trouble. The worst part for us is that so many people smoked at the time, and ventilation wasn't great, so we were breathing it all in. We didn't get any smokers of anything but tobacco!"

Rory Gallagher on Macroom Castle gates *Courtesy S McSweeney*

Evelyn Mungovan McSweeney

" I run McSweeney's Grocery and Sweet Shop on Main Street and the festival was a fantastic period for us. We'd be open until midnight. Milk would be delivered to outside our door, but was too tempting for misfortunate visitors who had little money and it would be gone by the time we opened at 8am. We solved the problem by giving the milkman a key! They were a grand crowd, no trouble. My husband left the keys in the car one night and they were still there the next day. That's an example of how decent people were.

We had sandwiches ready for them and they bought a lot of minerals, ice-cream and chocolate. Life was simpler then, fewer products, no pot noodles! They slept on the street in doorways, including ours, and we seem to have been very lucky with the weather so it was pleasant for them. It was a time of innocence and we all felt safe, though I must say that today in Macroom I feel perfectly safe at any time of the day or night.

I was involved in the youth club and we ran dances so we were used to having stars coming and going. The Mountain Dew Festival was still a big thing, though. I didn't get to many of the concerts as I was on duty all day and night. The Castle grounds were a great facility and it was great to be able to accommodate the Rory concert. All in all, the Macroom people went with the flow and gave people a chance and it paid off. "

Cork Examiner/Evening Echo

Kevin O'Brien

"I was a teacher in McEgan College during the years of the festival and didn't get involved unless I was asked to fall in from time to time. I helped to launch the 1,000 balloons at one of the openings and one of the most enjoyable moments for me was in 1977 when we had a bonfire on the Square in the town. We were delighted that we were allowed to have one (I'm not sure it would be permitted these days) and it was lovely to see everyone gather around it for a decent sing-song.

I was in the car with Rory Gallagher's band for the first of his concerts. Charlie Leonard was in charge of that operation and I just went along for the ride. I didn't say a word and I don't remember Lou Martin or others saying anything either! Rory was in the car in front of us. After the concert I bought Rory's cassette tape and he signed it for me. Thinking I could easily get another one, I gave it to someone in France. Of course I never got around to getting another one. I didn't get to the second of Gallagher's concerts as the festival date was changed by a few days and I had set the date for my wedding for then. I was tempted ...

I remember Lindisfarne playing after Van Morrison and stealing the show. I knew their stuff as I play the guitar and loved their 'Fog on the Tyne' song. Some people had gone away after Van Morrison as they assumed he was on last, but they missed the best band of the day. I loved Julie Felix too as when I was learning the guitar you could play it yourself like her. I liked that kind of stuff.

We all bought tickets for Love Machine. They were pure sexual glamour to us! I don't remember anything about the music!

The folk music day was tremendous value. Top acts all in one programme! In fairness, the organising committee went out of their way to cater to everybody, every taste, every age. They worked fierce hard. Michael Lynch designed the Rory Gallagher stage and did terrific work on it. I also remember seeing Martin Fitz-Gerald with his sleeves rolled up, sweating, helping to put up The Dome."

Bill Hennigan

"I was one of a team of twenty working on security for the first Rory concert and also for the 1981 one in Coolcower. For the first one I worked mainly in the Castle grounds, moving around with two others making sure people were coming through with tickets and generally keeping an eye on things. The weather was lovely, which helped.

I was very angry when I saw that shops and other premises closed up and weren't there to serve all the crowds. They had come from places like Portlaoise and were hungry. It really was a hindrance to have the Victoria Hotel close up and put covers on their windows. It was a total disgrace, a shame! And of course there was no trouble. Denis J Murray opened up his pub and the fans he let in for food and drink even cleared up the place afterwards, they were so grateful.

In 1981, there was a bit of trouble, security-wise. We were manning the front gates at Coolcower and the Gardaí came along. There was one particularly troublesome lad, so one of the guards took his shoes off him and drove him eight miles out of town to let him walk off whatever was wrong with him. The guard came back in the squad car, but by the time he got back the trouble-maker was ahead of him. He must have hitched a lift! Elvis Costello was brilliant, world class, and to think he came to Macroom!

I wasn't in a job in those days and was young and foolish. The festival was completely new to us and pushed us into situations out of the normal things that happened in Macroom. We were sorry it ended and we talked about it for months before it happened and then for months after, and we are still talking about it. It was brilliant!"

Elvis Costello *Cork Examiner/Evening Echo*

Donal O'Mahony

Rock festivals scare me! The music isn't my thing and wasn't even then. I was forty-five at the time of the first one and was Headmaster at McEgan College. We allowed the building to be used to feed the acts performing throughout the festivals. It was in their contracts that they would be provided with meals, so catering was done there. It looks like they demanded vodka too, as afterwards there were quite a few empty bottles around.

I remember that we had to make a huge number of sandwiches and sometime after one of the festivals it seemed all the vermin in the country was attracted to the remains dumped behind the college stage.

The Irish dancing competitions were held in the college too. These days insurance issues would stop you doing that. All in all we felt we were in the centre of the action, but on the day of the Rory Gallagher concert, I went to mass and saw all the denim jackets and jeans, teenagers lying down on the street, and headed out of town to keep away from it! The bloody music was terrible! Cork was playing Clare in Thurles. I went from the frying pan into the fire – 20,000 in Macroom to 40,000 in Thurles!

I know very little about drugs, even now in my eighties, and I knew less then,

but what I did recognise was that smell from burning incense sticks and some kind of candle, which I was told resembled hash. And I certainly smelled that around the streets.

I remember hearing about a crowd of young fellas in court charged with possession of drugs, the May after one of the first festivals. I can clearly picture a guy with checked trousers and a colourful cap, who was dressed just like a TV undercover cop of the time. He always seemed to be around. At one stage Martin Fitz-Gerald said to him, "For crying out loud, give us a break!"

I walked one day to the park down by the river and I saw all these people emerging from tents. They were only children, really. What a sight that was. I live on New Street, on the Killarney road and towards the end of one of the festivals I saw this fella thumbing. I asked him where he was going. "Sligo", he said. He somehow thought he could take a shortcut through Killarney. He could have ended up in Killorglin!

Marianne Faithfull was more in my sphere; I liked her. I was sorry when the festival ended. It shook up the place.

Cork Examiner/Evening Echo

The Last Word

Roz Crowley

All the recollections in this book are personal, and some of them may be remembered and seen through rose-tinted glasses and a desire to romanticise contributors' teenage and early twenties' years. Painting their pictures with words may also have diluted some of the sadness people feel that the festival is no more.

What was more obvious was the fun that came from being part of something new and exciting, something that was mysterious, energising and a little scary for all that.

There was gentle leadership, a nurturing of local management talents, a recognition of the grafting of many. If local businesses profited, all the better. If vocal minorities saw profit as a dirty word, it might have been better viewed as profits made meant profits spent in the community. If the lessons of Woodstock and Glastonbury had been studied, there could be nothing done by halves, and the energy that takes is costly, both financially and in terms of stamina.

Seven years of festivals was an enormous achievement, and for that time music lovers were exposed to some of the greatest talent the world has to offer, at a cost they could all afford. The next phase of concerts which followed in the wake of Macroom, indoor and outdoor, incurred the kind of running costs that today makes it prohibitive for many.

Macroom Mountain Dew Festival may have been a little rough around the edges, but those edges provided a relaxed aura, a local charisma, a tenor, a tone, a vibe that the musicians I interviewed said was unique to this festival, and which was reflected in those who attended it.

No-one disputes the fact that The Mountain Dew Festival put Macroom on the map. Forty years later, it remains a happy time for those who attended it, performed at it and worked and lived its seven years. Fortune certainly favoured the brave, and faith in the weather meant that, with tiny exceptional sprinkles of rain, the sun shone throughout.

The first open-air Rock concert in Ireland took its place in the nation's music history.

Index

Paul Brady Cork Examiner/Evening Echo

Acknowledgements

Roz Crowley is a freelance writer and editor, based near Blarney in Co. Cork. www.rozcrowley.com

Roz Crowley acknowledges, with thanks, the contribution of the photographers who went through their boxes of negatives of forty years ago to provide some pics which have never been seen before. The extensive help of members of the library and photographic staff of *The Irish Examiner* has been invaluable, especially Pauline Hallissey and Ciarán McCarthy, and *The Southern Star* and *The Longford Leader* who also gave permission to use extracts from their newspapers. Thanks to John Foyle and Ferdia McAnna for their help in contacting acts and to Mary Somers, Peter Somers, Dónal Gallagher, Nadine King, Paul Charles, Jonathan Nicholls, Catryn Power, enthusiastic friends, and all the interviewees who not only provided the words for this book, but also searched for photographs and press cuttings, often providing leads for further interviews. As always, the editorial team and designer deserve special thanks for their patience when last minute additions proved too hard to resist. Top of the list in all aspects of the book was John Martin Fitz-Gerald, without whose help this book would not have been written or published.

Thanks also to her family, especially husband Bill whose cooking skills have greatly improved since the start of this book.

Don Hall's piece on his father Frank Hall appears courtesy of the author and *The Southern Star* where it first appeared in 2015.

Extract from an article written by Rocky de Valera appeared in *In Dublin* in 1982.

Contributions from The Edge and Joe O'Herlihy appear courtesy of Ghost Blues documentary, Eagle Rock Entertainment.

Useful website: Rorygallagher.com

Rory Gallagher at Mountain Dew German recording:
https://www.youtube.com/watch?v=5E7hs5wzt2Y

Archive pictures from Cork Examiner/Evening Echo courtesy of Irish Examiner.

Cork Examiner/Evening Echo

Whoever means to shake off gloom
Let him repair to sweet Macroom,
For here his cares he will entomb
And think no more of sorrow.

John Connolly, 1774